LETTING PROPEH

SEAN ANDREWS

EDITOR: ROGER SPROSTON

Straightforward Guides
www.straightforwardco.co.uk

Straightforward Guides

978-1-913342-48-7

Printed by
4edge www.4edge.co.uk

Cover design by BW Studio Derby

Contents

The aim of this revised edition of Letting Property for Profit **(updated to 2020)** is to demonstrate in a clear and uncomplicated way the main considerations involved in developing and managing a residential property portfolio.

Although more stringent financial rules are deterring some landlords from investing in the rental sector and although it is getting harder for the would be landlord to gain access to the buy-to-let sector in the south east of England because of high prices, the opportunities for landlords to invest and make a decent return generally, in particular in the Midlands and North, are better than ever, with rents across Britain set to rise by more than 20% over the next five years and with more and more individuals and families moving into the private rented sector.

The Coronavirus Act 2020- temporary law changes

At the time of writing, we are in the middle of the coronavirus epidemic, and quite apart from the effect on the general public, housing is affected across the board. Housing sales and rentals have just got underway again after a brief suspension. Would-be property investors and potential landlords need to be aware of the changes, however temporary.

In relation to the management of property, the government has warned landlords that they are still legally obligated to carry out urgent health and safety repairs. However, it clarified that non-urgent repairs should be done at a later date, as agreed between tenants and landlords.

The government issued the following the guidance: "Landlords remain legally obligated to ensure properties meet the required standard – urgent, essential health and safety repairs should be made. An agreement for non-urgent repairs to be done later should be made between tenants and landlords. Local authorities are also encouraged to take a pragmatic, risk-based approach to enforcement."

The government said it is committed to supporting landlords as well as tenants. The statement added: "We have also agreed with lenders that they will ensure support is available where it is needed for landlords. "Landlords will also be protected by a three-month mortgage payment holiday where they have buy-to-let mortgages."

Landlords have been warned to take note of the upcoming Minimum Energy Efficiency Standard regulation coming into force on 1 April 2020. The changes mean properties where tenancies pre-date April 2018 have to have an Energy Performance Rating above E. When initially introduced in April 2018, all properties marketed for let were legally required to have an EPC (energy performance certificate) rating of E or above before the commencement of any new tenancies. However, the legislation will shortly be extended to also cover properties where current tenancies pre-date April 2018. Landlord regulatory requirements have not been relaxed during the coronavirus outbreak and financial penalties for non-compliance remain enforceable, with a potential fine of up to £5,000 per infraction. The government stated:

"Landlords should make every effort to ensure they are meeting at least the new minimum standards despite the logistical challenges imposed by the outbreak.

It is vital to maintain open channels of communication with tenants to ensure that they are not vulnerable or self-isolating before proceeding with any essential work."

All court possession orders have been suspended since March 2020. Hearings are due to start again at the end of September but evictions are banned in Scotland and Northern Ireland until March 2021. When hearings start again, the courts will prioritise cases of extreme arrears, anti-social behaviour and domestic violence. Landlords must also reactivate notices served before August 3rd 2020 in writing to tenants and the courts. Finally, if a landlord wants to serve a section 21 notice to repossess the property to sell it or live in it then they must give tenants 6 months notice, rather than the usual two.

A note of caution, as this situation is changing rapidly, for up to date advice on giving notice go to:

https://england.shelter.org.uk/housing_advice/coronavirus

The whole situation which has arisen due to COVID 19 has to be factored into the equation when deciding to go ahead and purchase property on a buy-to-let basis.

Overall, private letting of residential property has grown significantly in the last 25 years. However, in some cases those who are involved in letting property do not have the professional knowledge needed to manage effectively and often end up in a mess. Little thought is given to the fact that a complex framework of law covers the landlord and tenant, defining the relationship between the two.

This book covers the acquisition, letting and managing of property in depth and should enable the landlord, or potential landlord to develop a portfolio of properties and manage effectively and efficiently, at the same time protecting his or her asset, whether it be a house, flat or House in Multi-Occupation.

Also included in this edition is a detailed guide to landlords tax obligations, including capital gains tax and advice on how to minimize liability. This book is essential reading for any landlord, or potential landlord and should prove to be invaluable.

****

CHAPTER 1

INVESTING IN PROPERTY-POINTS TO CONSIDER

Investing in Property

The overall demand for private rented property is now stronger than ever, with the mortgage market restricted for purchasers and house price inflation, particularly in the south east, creating the need for high deposits which people cannot find. Lending has become far more stringent, owing to the banks unwillingness to loan money, particularly to property investors. Essentially, accessing finance has become a big issue. The banks favor those with large cash deposits. This is the same in the buy-to-let sector as for domestic mortgages.

However, if finance can be arranged then the yields that one can expect from buy-to-let properties are high by comparison, currently standing at 6% on average. Of course, this depends on where the property is located. See overleaf for tables indicating the best and worst buy to let areas in the UK. A yield is a portfolio's annual rental income as a percentage of total value. The reason is that demand for private rented property is high, particularly as first time buyers cannot get a toehold in the market. They are instead turning to the private rental sector. Therefore, investing in property, for the longer term, as opposed to investing for short-term gain, is still a viable option.

Best and worst buy to let areas in the UK

Landlords looking for the UK's best buy-to-let areas in **2020** should consider Liverpool and the North East of England, as well as Scotland. (bear in mind that these figures change over time and you should carry out your own research before buying).

- Liverpool's L1 postcode is currently the best place to buy-to-let in England, Scotland and Wales. It generates an impressive yield of 10 per cent, according to the new research. L1 is the main retail area, home to Liverpool One, as well as the commercial district and Chinatown
- it's followed by Falkirk's FK3 postcode and Glasgow's G52 postcode in Scotland. They produced an average investment return of 9.51 per cent and 8.71 per cent respectively
- the worst area for buy-to-let is in commuter town St Albans – its AL5 postcode produces a rental yield of just 1.95 per cent

Where are the best buy-to-let areas?

Sixteen of the top 25 postcodes are in the North West (predominantly Liverpool) and Scotland.

The North East also features prominently in the best areas for buy-to-let. TS1 and TS3 in Cleveland ranked fifth and twelfth respectively, while Sunderland features twice with SR8 and SR5, and Gateshead's NE8 is ranked eighteenth. See overleaf for 10 best areas in 2020.

The majority of the strongest postcodes in Britain have a yield of around 7 per cent. These include Leeds' LS2 at 7.92 per cent, Cardiff's CF43 at 7.61 per cent, Aberdeen's AB11 at 7.2 per cent, and Lancaster's LA14 at 7.06 per cent.

According to the research, here are the 10 best buy-to-let areas 2020:

Area	Rental yield
Liverpool, L1	10.00%
Falkirk, FK3	9.51%
Glasgow, G52	8.71%
Liverpool, L11	8.67%
Cleveland, TS1	8.50%
Kilmarnock, KA1	8.31%
Liverpool, L6	8.12%
Leicester, LE1	8.00%
Leeds, LS2	7.92%
Sheffield, S1	7.83%

The remaining postcodes in the top 25 best areas for buy-to-let are:

- Cardiff, CF43 (7.61 per cent)
- Cleveland, TS3 (7.60 per cent)
- Liverpool, L2 (7.56 per cent)
- Paisley, PA3 (7.45 per cent)
- Liverpool, L3 (7.40 per cent)
- Sunderland, SR8 (7.38 per cent)
- Glasgow, G51 (7.32 per cent)
- Gateshead, NE8 (7.27 per cent)
- Aberdeen, AB11 (7.20 per cent)
- Glasgow, G67 (7.20 per cent)
- Glasgow, G32 (7.13 per cent)
- Liverpool, L4 (7.13 per cent)
- Glasgow, G21 (7.10 per cent)
- Lancaster, LA14 (7.06 per cent)
- Sunderland, SR5 (6.99 per cent)

Where are the worst areas for buy-to-let?

The research found that many well-known commuter areas have the lowest yields. The lowest is AL5 in St Albans, where the average buying price is £800,000 and the average rent is £1,300, producing a yield of only 1.95 per cent. This puts it below London's W8 postcode (Kensington), which produces a return of 2.05 per cent. This is because average house prices are higher at almost £2 million. Other commuter spots in the bottom 10 areas for buy-to-let include RG10 in Reading, GU10 in Guildford, and KT7 in Kingston-upon-Thames. Sheffield has a postcode in both the top 10 (S1) and bottom 10 (S7). Also, Ipswich, as properties there have a median asking price of £397,500 and a rental value of £650.

Area	Rental yield
St Albans, AL5	1.95%
Ipswich, IP13	1.96%
Gloucester, GL6	2.03%
London, W8	2.05%
Birmingham, B73	2.18%
Sheffield, S7	2.19%
Kingston-upon-Thames, KT7	2.20%
Guildford, GU10	2.22%
Reading, RG10	2.26%
London, WC1X	2.28%

Rental yields

Investment properties which are rented out receive an income from tenants. In order to calculate the gross rental yield the annual rental income is divided by the purchase price of the property (annual rent÷price) X 100 = Gross rental yield). So, if the property was purchased for £75,000 (total) and the rent received is £450 per month the yield would be:

£5400 (annual rent) ÷ £75,000 X 100 which equals an annual yield of 7.2. This is a very respectable return on your capital. Of course if you are a landlord then you will want to factor in the costs of being a landlord, such as maintenance, insurance, loan costs, empty periods etc.

Capital yields

If and when a property increases with time, this is known as capital growth.

A simple example is if you buy a property for £75,000 and it increases by 25% there will be a capital appreciation of £18,750. It is a rule of thumb that low price properties might produce a high rental yield and low capital growth and vice-versa, although this is not always the case.

Again, each case differs and many factors will play a part but as long as you know what you want then you should be safe with your investment.

If you are interested in averages, landlords receive £899 in rent each month as a national average. However, as always, averages don't give the whole picture and vary by area. Landlords in London and the South East collect the highest rents, with £1,588 and £918 respectively (2018). In the west Midland rents average £678 and in the east of England £907. Approximately 60% of this is spent on borrowing and management costs, leaving landlords with a healthy 40% profit on average.

With buy-to-let mortgage rates so cheap (at the moment) now is the time to expand your portfolio releasing equity and raising deposits to buy new properties. However, when expanding your portfolio it is important to be realistic and ensure that you invest in properties that can be sold on easily, as there may come a time when you need to get your hands on the capital that you have tied up.

As with everything, property is a good investment as long as it is managed well. Too many would-be landlords buy property and neglect it which has a negative impact on the environment and also a negative impact on the investment as a whole. A run down property will decrease in value and the possibility of renting it out for a full market rent will also diminish. That is what this book is all about-how to become a good landlord and a good property manager and how to maximize the returns on your property.

What kind of property is suitable for letting?

Obviously there are a number of different markets when it comes to people who rent. There are those who are less affluent, young and single, in need of a sharing situation, but more likely to require more intensive management than older more mature (perhaps professional) people who can afford a higher rent but require more for their money. The type of property you have, its location, its condition, will very much determine the rent levels that you can charge and the clients that you will attract.

The type of rent that a landlord might expect to achieve will be percentage of the value of the freehold of the property, (or long leasehold in the case of flats). The eventual profit will be determined by the level of any existing mortgage and other outgoings.

If you are renting a flat it could be that it is in a mansion block or other flatted block and the service charge will need to be added to the rent. When letting a property it is necessary to consider profit after mortgage payments and likely tax bill plus other outgoings such as insurance and agents fees (if any). Of course there are other factors which make the profit achieved less important, that is the capital growth of the property. See further on in the book for a breakdown of taxation and allowances.

The importance of having a clear business plan

As a (would be) private landlord, a person considering letting a property for profit, or already doing so, it is vital that you are very clear about the following:

- What kind of approach do you intend to take as a landlord? Do you intend to purchase, or do you have, an up market property which you are going to rent out to stable professional tenants who will pay their rent on time and look after the property (hopefully!).
- What are the key factors that affect the value of a property in rental terms? Is the property close to public transport, does it have a garden, what floor is it on and what size are the rooms? Is it secure and in a crime free area? If you are acquiring a property you should set out what it is you are trying to achieve in the longer term, i.e. the type of person you want and match this to the likely residential requirements of that hypothetical person. You can then gain an idea of what type of property you are looking for, in what area, and you can then see whether or

not you can afford such a property. If not, you may have to change your plan.

- Do you intend to let to young single people, perhaps students, who will occupy individual rooms achieving higher returns but causing potentially greater headaches? Are you aware of the headaches? It is vitally important that you understand the ramifications of letting to different client groups and the potential problems in the future.

- Are you clear about the impact on the environment, and to other people, that your activities as a landlord may have? For example, do you have a maintenance plan which ensures that not only does your property look nice and remain well maintained but also takes into account whether the plan, or lack of it, will have an impact on the rest of the neighborhood? Will the type of tenant you intend to attract affect the rest of those living in the immediate vicinity

- What are the aims and objectives underpinning your business plan? Do you have a business plan or are you operating in an unstructured way? Taking into account the above, it is obviously necessary that you have a clear picture of the business environment that you intend to operate in, the legal and economic framework that governs and regulates the environment.

- It is vital that you are very clear about what it is you are trying to achieve. You should either understand the type of property that you already own or have an idea of the property you are trying to acquire to fit what client group. These goals should be very clear in your own mind and based on a long-term projection.

- Whether you are an existing property owner, or wish to acquire a property for the purpose of letting, the first objective is to formulate a business plan.

****

Chapter 2

COST CONSIDERATIONS WHEN DEVELOPING A PORTFOLIO OF BUY TO LET PROPERTIES

Budget

Before beginning to look for a house or flat for investment you need to sit down and give careful thought to the costs.

Deposit

Sometimes the estate agent (if you are buying through an estate agent) will ask you for a small deposit when you make the offer. This indicates that you are serious about the offer and is a widespread and legitimate practice, as long as the deposit is not too much. £100 is usual. However, this practice can vary. In London for example deposits can be quite a lot higher.

The main deposit for the property, i.e. the difference between the mortgage and what has been accepted for the property, isn't paid until the exchange of contracts. Once you have exchanged contracts on a property the purchase is legally binding. Until then, you are free to withdraw. The deposit cannot be reclaimed after exchange. Banks will normally lend up to 75 percent of the purchase price of the property for buy to let. However, the less you borrow the more favorable terms you can normally get from a bank or building society.

This particularly applies now, with the tightening of lending criteria. Also, the situation post Covid 19 will have a bearing on the banks willingness to lend due to the tenuous nature of the market.

Buy to Let Mortgages

Buy-to-let (BTL) mortgages are for landlords who buy property to rent out. The rules around buy-to-let mortgages are similar to those around regular mortgages, but there are some key differences. Read on for more information about how they work, how to get one and what mistakes to avoid.

Who can get a buy-to-let mortgage?
- You can get a buy-to-let mortgage if:
- You want to invest in houses or flats.
- You can afford to take a risk. Investing in property is risky, so you shouldn't take out a BTL mortgage if you can't afford to take that risk.
- You already own your own home. You'll struggle to get a buy-to-let mortgage if you don't already own your own home, whether outright or with an outstanding mortgage.
- You have a good credit record and aren't stretched too much on your other borrowings such as your existing mortgage and credit cards.
- You earn £25,000+ a year. Otherwise you might struggle to get a lender to approve your buy-to-let mortgage.
- You're under a certain age. Lenders have upper age limits, typically between 70 or 75. This is the oldest you can be when the mortgage ends not when it starts.

For example, if you are 45 when you take out a 25-year mortgage it will finish when you're 70.

How do buy-to-let mortgages work?

Buy-to-let mortgages are a lot like ordinary mortgages, but with some key differences:

- Interest rates on buy-to-let mortgages are usually higher.
- The fees also tend to be much higher.
- The minimum deposit for a buy-to-let mortgage is usually 25% of the property's value (although it can vary between 20-40%).
- Many BTL mortgages are interest-only. This means you don't pay anything each month, but at the end of the mortgage term you repay the capital in full.
- A significant proportion of BTL mortgage lending is not regulated by the Financial Conduct Authority (FCA).
- There are exceptions, for example, if you wish to let the property to a close family member (e.g. spouse, civil partner, child, grandparent, parent or sibling). These are often referred to as a consumer buy to let mortgages and are assessed according to the same strict affordability rules as a residential mortgage.

How much you can you borrow for buy-to-let mortgages

The maximum you can borrow is linked to the amount of rental income you expect to receive. Lenders typically need the rental income to be a 25–30% higher than your mortgage payment. To find out what your rent might be talk to local letting agents, or check the local press and online to find out how much similar properties are rented for.

Where to get a buy-to-let mortgage

Most of the big banks and some specialist lenders offer BTL mortgages. It's a good idea to talk to a mortgage broker before you take out a buy-to-let mortgage, as they will help you choose the most suitable deal for you.

Using price comparison websites

Comparison websites are a good starting point for anyone trying to find a mortgage tailored to their needs. the following are the most popular.

- Moneyfacts
- Money Saving Expert
- MoneySuperMarket
- Which?

Comparison websites won't all give you the same results, so make sure you use more than one site before making a decision. It is also important to do some research into the type of product and features you need before making a purchase or changing supplier.Don't assume that your property will always have tenants. There will almost certainly be 'voids' when the property is unoccupied or rent isn't paid and you'll need to have a financial 'cushion' to meet your mortgage payments. When you do have rent coming in, use some of it to top up your savings account.

You might also need savings for major repair bills. For example, the boiler might break down, or there may be a blocked drain.

Stamp Duty Land Tax (SDLT)for buy to let properties is an extra 3% on top of the current SDLT rate bands.

Stamp duty- What is stamp duty and who pays it?
Stamp Duty — Stamp Duty Land Tax (SDLT) official jargon — is a tax you pay when you buy a home. The buyer pays stamp duty – not the person selling. Stamp duty applies to both freehold and leasehold purchases over £125,000. The situation in Wales and Scotland is different and you should check the respective websites /www.gov.uk/guidance/sdlt-scottish-transactions and www.gov.uk/guidance/stamp-duty-land-tax-welsh-transactions. However, in England and Wales, additional property purchases attract a higher rate, as below:

The current rates of stamp duty from 1st April 2020 for buy to let (additional) properties are;
• 3% tax on the first £125,000
• 5% on the portion up to £250,000
• 8% on the portion up to £925,000
• 13% on the portion up to £1.5 million
• 15% on everything over that

Anyone buying a second property that isn't their main residence will be charged these new rates. This will include holiday lets and buying a property for children if the parents leave their name on the title deeds.

Stamp duty has to be paid within 14 days of completion of the purchase of the property (England and Wales)) although this is usually paid by the solicitor on completion. The amount of Stamp Duty paid is deductible from any capital gains you might make when the property is sold.

Special rates

There are different SDLT rules and rate calculations for:

- corporate bodies and people buying 6 or more residential properties in one transaction
- shared ownership properties
- multiple purchases or transfers between the same buyer and seller ('linked purchases')
- purchases that mean you own more than one property
- companies and trusts buying residential property

Tax for properties held offshore

HMRC announced in March 2013, that an annual levy will now be made on properties held in British and Offshore companies, costing £2million or more. This is a measure to tackle tax avoidance. Those homes valued at between £2m-£5m will have to pay £15,000 per year; those between £5m-£10m will be taxed at £35,000; those with values of between £10m-£20m will pay £70,000 per year. owners of homes above £20m per year will have to pay £140,000 per year. Whilst this is not likely to affect readers of this book, it is always better to be aware of such changes.

Other costs

A solicitor normally carries out conveyancing of property. However, individuals can do their own conveyancing, although it isn't as simple as it appears. All the necessary paperwork can be obtained from legal stationers and it is executed on a step-by-step basis.

It has to be said that solicitors are now very competitive with their charges and, for the sake of between £850-£1500 including

VAT, it is better to let someone else do the work which allows you to concentrate on other things. Another issue will be that your lender will not look favourably on you doing your own conveyancing and will usually insist on the use of a solicitor or licensed conveyancer..

Land Registry

The Land Registry records all purchases of land in England and Wales and is open to the public (inspection of records, called a property search). The registered title to any particular piece of land or property will carry with it a description and include the name of owner, mortgage, rights over other persons land and any other rights. There is a small charge for inspection. A lot of solicitors have direct links and can carry out searches very quickly. Not all properties are registered although it is now a duty to register all transactions.

Capital gains tax-buy to let property?

You pay capital gains tax on buy to let property if you sell the property for more than you paid for it after deducting costs such as stamp duty and estate agent/solicitors fees. By making a profit, you are essentially 'gaining capital', and so the tax applies.

However, as an individual you get an annual allowance to set against any gain. In the 2020/2021 tax year, this allowance is £12,000. This is a special allowance purely for capital items and is separate from the annual personal income tax allowance. If the gain is greater than the £12,000 allowance, you will pay tax at a rate of either 18% or 28% on that profit depending on the amount of income and capital gains you have.

Note that the lower CGT rates of 10% and 20% announced in the March 2016 budget do not apply to landlords and buy to let properties.

Private Residence Relief

Private residence relief (PRR) means homeowners selling their primary residence don't have to pay CGT on profits. This also applies to some extent to landlords who used to live in the property as their main residence, but are now selling it.

At present, you are exempt from paying tax on the final 18 months that you owned the property, regardless of whether or not it is rented out. This gives you longer to sell the property after moving out before you become eligible to pay capital gains tax.

From April 2020, this is expected to shorten to nine months, so once you have not lived in a property that was once your main residence for longer than nine months, you will probably need to pay some CGT on profits you make when you sell it.

Letting relief changes

For those who qualify for PRR, it might also be possible to claim letting relief. This relief can reduce the capital gains tax owed on a property by up to £40,000 of tax-free gains, or £80,000 for a couple. Letting relief can currently be claimed if you used to live in the property you are selling, and have also let out part or all of it for residential accommodation. You can claim the lowest of the following: the same as the amount of PRR you will receive; £40,000; the chargeable gain you make from the period you let out the property. When the new rules come in from April 2020, you will only be able to claim this relief if you live there when it is being sold – if you share occupancy with your tenant.

Deductions and exceptions

Under current rules – and with no expectation of this changing – there are certain costs that can be deducted from your CGT. This includes:

- Stamp duty paid on purchase of property
- Estate agent fees
- Solicitor fees
- Improvement costs (such as extensions)
- Qualifying buying and selling costs (such as surveyor fees)

Aside from this, capital gains tax is only payable on property that is owned by individuals. Where property is owned by a limited company, which is becoming an increasingly popular method to run property investments, corporation tax is applied instead. Corporation tax is currently 19%,.

Energy Performance Certificates-When should you get an EPC?

As a general rule, an EPC is required every time a home is put up for sale or for rent. So, a newly constructed home will have one, a landlord will need one to show potential tenants, and a seller must have one to show to potential buyers. There are a few exceptions. You don't need one for a room that's being rented out by a resident landlord and listed buildings may also be exempt as they can't have upgrades like double glazing.

The requirement for an EPC has been the law since 2008 (2009 in Scotland), meaning that if your home has been let or sold since then it should have one. They remain valid for 10 years. There's a national register of EPCs, unless you've opted out, where you can take a look at your property's previous certificates (as well as viewing similar properties in your neighbourhood for a comparison of how energy efficient your home is).

Do I need to buy an EPC when buying or renting a property?
You should never be charged for an EPC when you're looking to buy or rent, it should be handed over free of charge — otherwise the seller or landlord could be fined £200. If you're a landlord or seller, you'll need to at least get this certificate ordered before you put the property on the market (you may be able to use the EPC given to you when you bought the property if it's still valid). If you own a commercial property that you want to sell or lease, you'll also need to get an EPC organised. If you're interested in the energy performance of your existing home, and don't match the eligibility criteria mentioned above, there is nothing stopping you from getting one commissioned for your home for personal use – but you will have to pay for it.

How much does an EPC cost?
There's no fixed fee for an EPC, it depends on a number of factors including what kind of property you live in and how many bedrooms it has. The area you live in can also affect the price considerably.

EPC prices typically start at £35, but a certificate for a large house in an expensive city could easily cost several times that.

What information is displayed on an EPC?

An EPC is a relatively straightforward certificate. It will look a bit like the multi-coloured sticker that you get on new household appliances. the EPC includes:

Energy efficiency rating

A section of your EPC will be dedicated to how energy efficient your property is. It's graded from A to G, with A meaning an energy efficient, well-insulated, probably modern home, and G meaning a draughty old building where the wind rattles the walls. Typically, you'll find an older property with no retrofitted energy-saving technology will be around a D grade. There will also be a number from 1 – 100, where a higher number signifies that the home is more efficient and the fuel bills will cost less.

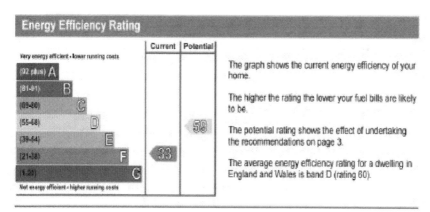

Estimated costs of running your home

Your EPC will give an indication of how much it will cost to heat and power your home. Details are also listed on potential savings that could be made should you improve the energy efficiency of your household running costs.

Estimated energy costs of this home

	Current costs	Potential costs	Potential future savings
Lighting	£375 over 3 years	£207 over 3 years	You could save £2,865 over 3 years
Heating	£4,443 over 3 years	£2,073 over 3 years	
Hot water	£549 over 3 years	£222 over 3 years	
Totals:	£5,367	£2,502	

These figures show how much the average household would spend in this property for heating, lighting and hot water. This excludes energy use for running appliances like TVs, computers and cookers, and any electricity generated by microgeneration.

Summary of energy performance related features

This section of the EPC will give you an indication of how energy efficient different aspects of your home are. It can act as a useful guide to help you work out which areas to focus on first when improving your home's efficiency.

Summary of this home's energy performance related features

Element	Description	Energy Efficiency
Walls	Cavity wall, as built, partial insulation (assumed)	★★★☆☆
Roof	Pitched, 75 mm loft insulation	★★★☆☆
Floor	Solid, no insulation (assumed)	--
Windows	Partial double glazing	★★☆☆☆
Main heating	Boiler and radiators, mains gas	★★★☆☆
Main heating controls	Programmer, room thermostat and TRVs	★★★★☆
Secondary heating	None	--
Hot water	From main system	★★★☆☆
Lighting	Low energy lighting in 17% of fixed outlets	★★☆☆☆

Current primary energy use per square metre of floor area: 298 kWh/m² per year

Changes to EPCs for landlords and tenants

From April 2020, under the Minimum Energy Efficiency Standards

(MEES) landlords will be required to achieve a minimum rating of E on the EPC for their rental property. Unless there is an accepted exemption, landlords face a penalty of up to £4,000 for failure to meet the minimum efficiency requirement. The information provided on EPCs is also helpful for tenants looking to improve the energy efficiency of their home. As of April 2016, tenants can seek permission from their landlord to undertake energy efficiency measures on their privately rented property.

Who can carry out an EPC?

An accredited domestic energy assessor will need to issue you with your EPC, it's not something you can do by yourself. You might be offered the services of one via an estate agent or letting agent, but you can find your own if you prefer or want to compare prices. You can also visit the EPC Register for recommendations.

Structural surveys

The basic structural survey is the homebuyers' survey and valuation, which is normally carried out by the building society or other lender and it will cost you between £200-350 and is not really an in-depth survey, merely allowing the lender to see whether they should lend or not and how much they should lend. Sometimes lenders keep what they refer to as a retention, which means that they will not forward the full value (less deposit) until certain defined works have been carried out.

If you want to go further than a homebuyers report, then you will have to instruct a firm of surveyors who have several survey types, depending on how far you want to go and how much you want to spend.

A word of caution. Many people go rushing headlong into buying a flat or house. If you stop and think about this, it is complete folly and can prove very expensive later. A house or flat is a commodity like other commodities, except that it is usually a lot more expensive. A lot can be wrong with the commodity that you have purchased which is not immediately obvious. Only after you have completed the deal and paid over the odds for your purchase do you begin to regret what you have done.

The true market price of a property is not what the estate agent is asking, certainly not what the seller is asking. The true market price is the difference between what a property similar to the one in good condition is being sold at and your property minus cost of works to bring it up to that value. Therefore, if you have any doubts whatsoever, and if you can afford it, get a detailed survey of the property you are proposing to buy and get the works that are required costed out.

When negotiating, this survey is an essential tool in order to arrive at an accurate and fair price. Do not rest faith in others, particularly when you alone stand to lose.

One further word of caution. As stated, a lot of problems with property cannot be seen. A structural survey will highlight those. In some cases it may not be wise to proceed at all.

Mortgage arrangement fees

Depending upon the type of mortgage you are considering you may have to pay an arrangement fee. You should budget for anything up to 2% of the purchase price.

Chapter 3

FINDING SUITABLE PROPERTY TO BUY

Having looked at the costs of acquiring a property, we need now to look at the type of property that you might want to invest in and also the areas that you should look in. Obviously, where you choose to buy your property will be your own decision. However, it may be your first time and you may be at a loss as to where to buy, i.e. rural areas or urban areas, the type and cost of property or whether a house or flat. There are several considerations here. The main consideration for a buy-to-let property is the letting potential and security of your asset, i.e. will it appreciate or will it depreciate. As mentioned in the previous chapter, flats are a better investment than houses, as a rule of thumb.

Area

Buying in a built up area has its advantages and disadvantages. There is usually more demand for property in a built up area. As far as letting is concerned, there are obvious advantages in that there are normally more close communities, because of the sheer density. Local services are closer to hand and there is a greater variety of housing for sale. Transport links are also usually quite good and there are normally plenty of shops.

Disadvantages are less space, less privacy, more local activity, noise and pollution, less street parking and more expensive insurance.

There are also different schooling environments to rural environments. Although the incidence of crime and vandalism and levels of overall stress are higher in built up, more urban areas, this is not the case with all built up areas. It is up to the buyer to carry out research before making a commitment.

If you are thinking of buying to let in a rural area, you might want to consider the following:

- There is more detached housing with land, more space and privacy.
- There is also cleaner air and insurance premiums can be lower.
- Disadvantages can be isolation, loneliness, lower level of services generally, limited choice of local education, therefore the property will be harder to let.

Choosing your property

You should think carefully when considering purchasing a larger property. You may encounter higher costs prior to letting, and also costs that may deter the would be tenant, which may include:

- Larger more expensive carpeting.
- More furniture. If you are letting your property furnished then you will need to outlay more at the outset.
- Larger gardens to tend. Although this may have been one of the attractions, large gardens are time consuming, expensive and hard work.
- Bigger bills plus more decorating and higher overall maintenance costs.

Purchasing a flat

There are some important points to remember when purchasing a flat. These are common points that are overlooked. For example, if you are buying a flat in a block that is leasehold you will need permission to sublet. This may pose difficulties depending on the freeholder. In addition, the type of cladding on blocks of flats is crucial.

Cladding on blocks

Purchasers beware-New advice on cladding applies to all blocks, not only high-rises.

If a person owns a flat of any height with any type of cladding, or none at all, new safety advice on external walls means that the owners of privately owned flats in England could face months of "cladmin" before being able to sell or remortgage. If you intend to buy a flat then you should be aware of the cladding issue. Since government advice was extended to blocks of all heights last month, buyers have been pulling out of sales in low-rise blocks, as well as high-rise.

What fire report do you need?

The government has issued new advice in response to the Grenfell fire in 2017. Building owners must ensure that blocks of any height are safe. Mortgage lenders require a report, for which fire engineers cut holes in building to check wall systems.

Fewer than 500 engineers have the indemnity insurance for this. Cladding and insulation samples are tested to check they match the building's design.

If any are combustible the system is deemed safe if a three-storey replica wall passes a fire test. The wait for a test can be eight months to a year. The cost, typically £10,000 to £45,000, is split between all flat owners in the block. The Royal Institution of Chartered Surveyors, the Building Societies Association and UK Finance have launched an external wall system form (EWS1). valid for five years.

What if walls are found unsafe?
The new guidance affects buildings with any flammable cladding or insulation, not only the type that was on Grenfell Tower. Building owners must check that fire breaks are correctly fitted inside walls. In 98 per cent of cases where surveyors have removed cladding to inspect this they have found defects.

Who pays for remediation?
Under leasehold law, flat owners are liable. The typical bill is from £20,000 a flat. The government has a £200 million fund to fix private flats with aluminium composite material (ACM), like that on Grefell Tower, 93 blocks qualify. It does not cover other materials, such as timber. Developers or freeholders are paying at another 77 ACM blocks. If the development was completed less than ten years ago leaseholders may be able to claim under the new-home warranty.

Service charge
If you purchase a flat in a block, the costs of maintenance of the flat will be your own. However, the costs of maintaining the common parts will be down to the landlord (usually) paid for by you through

a service charge. There has been an awful lot of trouble with service charges, trouble between landlord and leaseholder. It has to be said that many landlords see service charges as a way of making profit over and above other income, which is usually negligible after sale of a lease. Many landlords will own the companies that carry out the work and retain the profit made by these companies. They will charge leaseholders excessively for works, which are often not needed.

The 1996 Housing Act, amended by the 2002 Commonhold and Leasehold Reform Act, attempts to strengthen the hand of leaseholders against unscrupulous landlords by making it very difficult indeed for landlords to take legal action for forfeiture (repossession) of lease without first giving the leaseholder a chance to challenge the service charges. In addition, the Acts place an obligation on landlords to be more transparent by producing more detailed accounts and information.

Be very careful if you are considering buying a flat in a block. You should establish levels of service charges and look at accounts. Try to elicit information from other leaseholders. It could be that there is a leaseholders organisation, formed to manage their own service charges. This will give you direct control over contracts such as gardening, cleaning, maintenance contracts and cyclical decoration contracts. Better value for money is obtained in this way. In this case, at least you know that the levels will be fair, as no one leaseholder stands to profit. All of the above should be considered as the profit that you make from letting your property can be greatly diminished by extra costs such as maintenance charges to a freeholder.

Ground rents

In the light of the recent problems highlighted in Parliament concerning escalating ground rents, rendering properties virtually un-sellable, be very careful about the provisions in a lease concerning annual (or other period) ground rent increases. Always take legal advice from a solicitor unconnected to the freeholder. Related to this is the fact that The Ministry of Housing, Communities and Local Government is preparing to call time on ground rents under the 2021-2023 Help to Buy Scheme, reducing ground rents to a peppercorn ground rent, in other words a few pounds a year..

Leasehold Reform Act 1993

Under this Act, as amended by The Commonhold and Leasehold Reform Act 2002, all leaseholders have the right to extend the length of their lease by a term of 90 years. For example, if your lease has 80 years left to run you can extend it to 170 Years. There is a procedure in the above Act for valuation. Leaseholders can collectively also purchase the freehold of the block.

There is a procedure for doing this in the Act although it is often time consuming and can be expensive. There are advantages however, particularly when leaseholders are not satisfied with management.

Viewing properties

Hopefully, by the time of reading, the Coronavirus restrictions on viewing properties will be over. Before you start house hunting, draw up a list of characteristics you will need from a property, such as the number of bedrooms, size of kitchen, garage and study and garden. Take the estate agents details with you when viewing. Also, take a tape measure with you.

Assess the location of the property. Look at all the aspects and the surroundings. Give some thought as to the impact this will have on the ability to rent.

Assess the building. Check the facing aspect of the property, i.e., north, south etc. Check the exterior carefully.

Look for a damp proof course - normally about 15cm from the ground. Look for damp inside and out. Items like leaking rainwater pipes should be noted, as they can be a cause of damp. Look carefully at the windows. Are they rotten? Do they need replacing and so on. Look for any cracks. These should most certainly be investigated. A crack can be symptomatic of something worse or it can merely be surface. If you are not in a position to make this judgment then others should make it for you.

Heating is important. If the house or flat has central heating you will need to know when it was last tested. Gas central heating should be tested at least once a year. All in all you need to remember that you cannot see everything in a house, particularly on the first visit.

A great deal may be being concealed from you. In addition, your own knowledge of property may be slim. A second opinion is a must.

Buying a listed building
Buildings of architectural or historical interest are listed by the Secretary of State for National Heritage following consultation with English Heritage, to protect them against inappropriate alteration.

In Wales, buildings are listed by   the Secretary of State for Wales in consultation with CADW (Heritage Wales). In Scotland, they are listed by the Secretary of State for Scotland, in consultation with Historic Scotland.

If you intend to carry out work to a listed building, you are likely to need listed building consent for any internal or external work, in addition to planning permission. The conservation officer in the local planning department can provide further information.

Buildings in conservation areas

Local authorities can designate areas of special architectural or historical significance. Conservation areas are protected to ensure that their character or interest is retained. Whole towns or villages may be conservation areas or simply one particular street.

Strict regulations are laid down for conservation areas. Protection includes all buildings and all types of trees that are larger than 7cm across at 1.5m above the ground. There may be limitations for putting up signs, outbuilding or items such as satellite dishes. Any developments in the area usually have to meet strict criteria, such as the use of traditional or local materials.

This also applies to property in national parks, designated areas of outstanding natural beauty and the Norfolk or Suffolk Broads. Whether or not a property is listed or is deemed to be in a conservation area will show up in a search.

Buying a new house

There are a number of benefits to buying a new house. You have the advantages of being the first owner. There should not be a demand for too much maintenance or DIY jobs, as the building is new.

There will however be a defects period, which usually runs for 6 months for building and 12 months for electrical mechanical. During this period you should expect minor problems, such as cracking of walls, plumbing etc, which will be the responsibility of the builder. Energy loss will be minimal. A new house today uses 50 per cent less energy than a house built 15 years ago; consider the savings over an older property. An energy rating indicates how energy efficient a house is.

The National House Building Council uses a rating scheme based on The National Energy Services Scheme, in which houses are given a rating between 0 and 10. A house rated 10 will be very energy efficient and have very low running costs for its size. In addition, an Energy Performance Certificate is mandatory, as described earlier.

Security and safety are built in to new houses, smoke alarms are standard and security locks on doors and windows are usually included. When the housing market is slow, developers usually offer incentives to buyers, such as cash back, payment of deposit etc.

Always check the freehold transfer concerning charges such as ground rent and service charges.

Building Guarantees

All new houses should be built to certain standards and qualify for one of the building industry guarantees. These building guarantees are normally essential for you to obtain a mortgage and they also make the property attractive to purchasers when you sell. A typical guarantee is the National House Building Council Guarantee (NHBCG).

The process of buying a property

Having considered the costs of the acquisition of a property, the next step is to find the property you want.

For the investor, as well as all the considerations listed below, the return on investment will be a key priority. Looking for a property is a long and sometimes dispiriting process. Trudging around estate agents, sorting through mountains of literature, dealing with estate agents details, scouring the papers and walking the streets. However, most of us find the property we want at the end of the day. It is then that we can put in our offer. In the times of coronavirus and beyond, estate agents are increasingly reverting to video footage to carry out virtual viewings.

Making an offer

You should put your offer in to the estate agent or direct to the seller, depending on who you are buying from. As discussed earlier, your offer should be based on sound judgment, on what the property is worth and how much rental income after costs that you can derive from it, not on your desire to secure the property at any cost. A survey will help you to arrive at a schedule of works and cost. If you cannot afford to employ a surveyor from a high street firm then you should try to enlist other help. In addition, you should take a long and careful look at the house yourself, not just a cursory glance. Look at everything and try to get an idea of the likely cost to you of rectifying defects.

However, I cannot stress enough the importance of getting a detailed survey. Eventually, you will be in a position to make an offer for the property. You should base this offer on sound judgment. You should make it clear that your offer is subject to contract and survey (if you require further examination or wish to carry out a survey after the offer).

Exchange of contracts

Once the buyer and seller are happy with all the details stated in the contract and your conveyancer can confirm that there are no outstanding legal queries, there will be an exchange of contracts. The sale is now legally binding for both parties. You should arrange the necessary insurances, buildings and contents from this moment on, as you are now responsible for the property.

Completing a sale

This is the final day of the sale and normally takes place around ten days after exchange. Exchange and completion can take place on the same day if necessary but this is unusual. On the day of completion, you are entitled to vacant possession and you will receive the keys.

****

Chapter 4

LOOKING TO BUY AT AUCTION

Although many people will go through the traditional route of acquiring buy-to-let property through an estate agent, there are other routes, one main one being the auction. The below describes the auction process as it should be, in normal times, post Covid19.

Buying at auction requires a different set of skills and you need to know what you are buying, where it is and what the problems are, if any. Why is it being sold at auction? Certainly, you need to act fairly quickly as you need to inspect the property before auction day, arrive at the final bid price that you will not exceed and be prepared to complete within 28 days.

What is a property auction?

The process is very similar to the normal method of private sale. However, for an auction sale the seller and their solicitor carry out all the necessary paperwork and legal investigations prior to the auction. Subject to the property receiving an acceptable bid, the property will be 'sold' on auction day with a legally binding exchange of contracts and a fixed completion date.

Different types of property auction houses

Auction houses vary in size and the amount of business that they conduct and the frequency with which they hold auctions. Most will sell both residential and commercial property and each will have its own style of operation, and fee structure. Large auction houses will hold auctions frequently, perhaps every two months and will have around 250 lots for sale.

A lot of the auctions happen in London but will also be held nearer to home. Most of the large auction houses will deal with property put forward by large institutions, such as banks selling repossessions and also local authorities and will advertise the sales in the mainstream media and trade papers. The medium size auction houses will hold auctions as frequently as they can, in regional venues, such as racecourses and conference centres, and depending on stock, usually every two to three months, tending to advertise locally. The small auction houses will have far fewer lots and will hold their sales in smaller local venues. They may advertise in local press but more often will trade on word of mouth.

Those who attend auctions
As you might imagine, all sorts of people attend auctions. The common denominator is that they are all interested in buying property.

Property investors are most common at auction, people who are starting out building a portfolio or those who have large portfolios that they wish to expand. They tend to fall into two groups, those who are after capital appreciation, i.e. buy at a low value and build the capital value and those who are looking for rental income. Then there are the property traders who like a quick profit from buying and 'flipping' property. These types usually have intimate knowledge of an area and are well placed to make a quick profit.

Then we have the developers who look for small profitable sites or larger sites where property can be built and sold on. The sites can have existing buildings on them or can be vacant lots with or without planning permission. Last, but not least, we have those people who intend to buy solely for the purpose of owner occupation, look to buy a below- value property that they can redesign and make their own.

What types of property are suitable for auction?

There is strong demand for all types of properties offered at auction. These may be properties requiring updating, those with short leases, development sites with or without planning permission, repossessions, forced sales, investment properties, ground rents, probates, receivership sales and local authority properties.

However, any type of property can be sold at auction and initially the property will be inspected to discuss specific criteria and the current situation. Extensive research will be carried out by the auction house and advice offered as to whether auction is the appropriate method of sale. The below represents a cross section of what might be found at auction.

Properties for Improvement

Properties in need of updating make ideal auction Lots. They are in great demand from refurbishment specialists and private buyers, keen to undertake a project for their own occupation or for resale. They also appeal to buy-to-let investors who carry out the improvements then retain them as part of a property portfolio.

Tenanted Properties

Residential houses and flats with tenants in residence sell well at auction. Notice doesn't need to be served on tenants, and rental income continues to be received right up to completion.

Residential Investments

Houses in multiple occupation and blocks of flats are sold at auction as valuable investments. Here it is the rent level that determines the sale price, just as much as the building itself.

Development Propositions

Derelict or disused farm buildings, empty commercial premises, buildings with potential for conversion or change of use, can all sell well at auction. In some locations a change to residential can significantly add to the value of a property, in other situations there may be space for additional dwellings or to substantially enlarge the property.

Building Land

There is no better way of ensuring a seller achieves best price for a building plot or parcel of development land than to offer it for sale by auction. Builders will be able to consult with architects, planners etc., and be ready to bid in the auction room.

Mixed-Use Properties

Properties that have twin uses or a variety of potential future uses are ideal for sale by auction. Retail shops with accommodation above appeal to investors as well as owner-occupiers.

Further conversion work can often be undertaken and the property tailored to suit the purchaser's special requirements.

Commercial Investments

Retail shops, offices, industrial units, garage blocks and parking areas - an ever increasing number of commercial investments are being sold at auction. It doesn't matter whether they are vacant or tenanted, with lease renewal soon needed or with a long way to run.

Unique Properties

There are always some rare entries, sought after property and prime locations that need to be sold in a competitive bidding environment. Unexpectedly high prices have been achieved by this route.

Amenity Land and Other Property

Paddocks, meadows, fields, moorings, amenity land and also other unusual land parcels are all sold at auction. If it is property or land that is surplus to requirements, the likelihood is a buyer can be found at auction.

Why is property being sold at an auction?

There are a number of reasons why property is sold at an auction:
A quick sale is needed, often due to the owner being in financial difficulties or it is a repossession

- There are structural problems which prevent the property being sold easily in the conventional manner.

- Properties sold by public bodies. Here you get all sort of property, including weird and wonderful properties such as public toilets and police stations, all of which may have their uses.
- The property is unique and there are no direct comparisons, such as lighthouses and the above mentioned public toilet.

It is always best to find out why exactly the property is being sold at auction. Is it so difficult to get rid of because of some inherent reason? Ask why is this property at auction and not being sold in the conventional way? Who exactly is the vendor and what if any are the problems stopping it being sold conventionally? The reasons that the property is at auction may be entirely innocent but it is always worth finding out to avoid future problems.

What happens next?
Once you have found your auction, to receive a complimentary auction catalogue you should contact the Auctioneers and this will give the information about the properties being offered for sale. You can also download a catalogue from the auctioneers website. The catalogue includes descriptions of the available properties, legal information, viewing arrangements and a guide price, which is purely an indication of a realistic selling price. This should not be taken as a firm asking or selling price and should be relied upon as a guide only. Professional advice must be taken in relation to any lot in which there is an interest.

For lots where viewings are arranged, these are carried out on a block basis and are published in all advertising and in the auction catalogue.

Any prospective purchaser is welcome at these viewings and should the scheduled appointments be inconvenient, alternative arrangements can be made. Any interest must be registered with the Auctioneers in order that prospective purchasers may be kept informed as to the progress of the sale.

Bidding for a property

The lots will be offered and the bidding taken to the highest possible level and once the gavel falls, the contracts will be exchanged. The buyer purchases the property at the price they bid - this cannot be negotiated and the stipulated terms cannot be changed. The buyer will then pay 10% of the purchase price on the day and completion occur 28 days later. The funds are then paid to the seller less the fees of the Auctioneers and those of the seller's solicitor.

The atmosphere of an auction room can be extremely exciting and competitive and it is often the case that an interested party will bid in excess of the figure that had previously been set as their maximum. In some cases, the prices achieved at auction can be higher than those achieved by private treaty. The seller will provide a legal pack that may be inspected at any time.

Auctioneers will strongly advise that professional advice is obtained from a legal representative. Details of the seller's solicitors will be available and, should a mortgage be required, it is advisable to have this in place prior to the sale. Again, Auctioneers strongly advise that funding is discussed with a professional advisor prior to attending the sale.

The successful buyer will be required to pay 10% of the purchase price on the day, together with a buyer's premium which is normally £250 including VAT. The balance of the purchase price is required on the agreed completion day and this is normally 28 days after the auction, however this can vary so best to check with the auction house.

finding out legal and survey information

A legal pack is requested from each of the vendor's solicitors and this contains copies of all legal papers, which will be required by any prospective purchasers for them to make an informed decision regarding the purchase of any lot. The pack will include office copy entries and plans, the relevant local authority search, leases (if applicable), Special Conditions of Sale, replies to pre-contract enquiries and any other relevant documents. A copy of these legal packs can usually be obtained from auctioneers for a small charge. Should any additional information be required, the seller's solicitors are listed in the catalogue and can be contacted directly. All legal packs are available for inspection at each auction. Any purchase at auction takes place under the assumption that documentation and the terms of the contract have been read. It is strongly recommended that any potential purchasers carry out full investigations for any lot in which they have an interest and a survey is an integral part of that investigation.

How is finance arranged?

Should a mortgage be required, approval in principle must be obtained prior to auction. Lenders are now familiar with the auction process and are usually willing to provide a mortgage offer for buyers intending to purchase at auction. A valuation and survey will be required along with legal evidence that there are no issues that will affect the value.

It is essential that the lender can provide funds within the timescale for completion. On the day of the auction, the purchaser will need to pay 10% of the purchase price and must ensure there are cleared funds to pay this amount. Sometimes, finance can be arranged through an Auctioneers on request.

Can lots be bought before auction?

Vendors may consider offers submitted before auction day. Any such offers need to be submitted in writing to an Auctioneers - this will be referred to the vendor and their instruction will be passed on to the prospective purchaser. Any offers will have to be unconditional and the buyer must be in a position to exchange contracts and pay the required deposit before auction day. With most auctioneers, no offers are considered within five days of the auction.

What should I take with me to the auction room?

The items required are as follows:

- Deposit cheque or banker's draft for any potential purchase
- Identification - this is legally required under the money laundering regulations. Therefore a driving licence or passport is required and a current utility bill to show proof of residence.

- Details of solicitors acting on behalf of any potential purchaser.

What happens if a prospective purchaser is unable to attend the auction?

If prospective purchasers are unable to attend the sale, it is possible to bid in other ways:

- By telephone - the interested party will be telephoned as the lot is being auctioned.
- By proxy in writing - a member of the auction team will represent the buyer, who has previously specified their maximum bid

In each case a registration form and cheque to cover the deposit and buyer's fee, are required prior to the date of the auction. A bidder's registration form is printed in the catalogue or alternatively can be obtained from the office

Will the property be insured when I purchase?

No - the purchaser at auction is responsible for obtaining Building insurance cover from the moment the property is deemed sold to them at auction.

Bidding from your smartphone

A new e'Bay for home buyers' is already big business making it easy to bid and buy via smartphone.

Homeowners wary of the auction room when it comes to buying or selling might prefer a new digital online auction called BidX1 (bidx1.com). It is a bit like online goods market eBay but for property – and the latest sale is today.

Difficulties of raising finance, bargains that turn into bottomless pits, fears about losing deposits, overbidding, and auctioneers plucking "2 bids off the wall" still put many off the traditional "ballroom" auction. But BidX1, up and running in the UK for 18 months, could be modifying that image. Most significant is the holding of a £4,500 "buyers fee" at registration to enable you to bid. If you win with the highest bid, you must pay a 10 per cent deposit at once and complete the purchase in 20 business days, possibly extended if over Christmas. Each time a highest bid is made, the auction automatically extends for a further minute and only closes when there are no further bids. BidX1's registration system for buyers and sellers complies with UK money laundering regulations and enables both sides to see on-screen who is bidding, how much, and when. BidX1's system can also see where the bid is from geographically and on what sort of device it was made. Customers can view, bid, buy and sell from home on a mobile phone. And it seems the detailed knowledge and visibility of who is bidding what, is of interest to both residential and commercial buyers and sellers because records can be checked. BidX1's fees are one-and-a- half to two-and-a half per cent of the sale price, depending on the sale and complexity of what's offered.

Chapter 5

FINDING TENANTS AND SUBSEQUENT MANAGEMENT OF YOUR PROPERTY

Whether you are either a landlord or a would - be landlord, you will need to source a tenant for your property. the choice of tenant will be crucial to the success of your business and also for your peace of mind.

Letting Agents

An amendment to the Enterprise and Regulatory Reform Act 2013 enabled the Government to require agents to sign up to a redress scheme. The Redress Scheme for Lettings Agency Work and Property Management Work (Requirement to Belong to a Scheme etc) (England) Order 2014 made membership of a scheme a legal requirement with effect from 1 October 2014. The Government also amended the Consumer Rights Act 2015 to require letting agents to publish a full tariff of their fees. (it should be noted that, If you intend to use an agent to manage your properties then ensure that it is signed up to a redress scheme. One such scheme is The Property Ombudsman Scheme. www.tpos.co.uk.

The Tenant Fees Act 2018 bans most letting fees and caps tenancy deposits paid by tenants in the private rented sector in England.

The ban on tenant fees applies to new or renewed tenancy agreements signed on or after 1 June 2019. From May 2020 it extends to all tenancies.

The government guidance on the Act for tenants, landlords and letting agents helps explain how this legislation affects them. You might also find the 'How to Rent' and 'How to Let' guides useful.

The aim of the Act is to reduce the costs that tenants can face at the outset, and throughout, a tenancy. Tenants will be able to see, at a glance, what a given property will cost them in the advertised rent with no hidden costs.

The party that contracts the service – the landlord – will be responsible for paying for that service, helping ensure the fees charged reflect the real economic value of the services provided and sharpen letting agents' incentive to compete for landlords' business. Local enforcement authorities have primary responsibility for enforcing this legislation. The Tenant Fees Act created an independent lead enforcement authority to provide advice and information to local authorities on the Act. Bristol city council has been appointed as the lead enforcement authority for lettings.

From 1 June 2019, the only payments that landlords or letting agents can charge to tenants in relation to new contracts are:

- rent
- a refundable tenancy deposit capped at no more than 5 weeks' rent where the total annual rent is less than £50,000, or 6 weeks' rent where the total annual rent is £50,000 or above
- a refundable holding deposit (to reserve a property) capped at no more than 1 week's rent

- payments associated with early termination of the tenancy, when requested by the tenant
- payments capped at £50 (or reasonably incurred costs, if higher) for the variation, assignment or novation of a tenancy
- payments in respect of utilities, communication services, TV licence and Council Tax
- a default fee for late payment of rent and replacement of a lost key/security device giving access to the housing, where required under a tenancy agreement

Online lettings agents

The rise of online lettings agents has been rapid and they now account for a growing percentage of the market. The attractions are obvious, the costs. One of the biggest online property agents,

EasyProperty.com offers 'pick and mix' services ranging from £10 a week for adverts on Right Move, Prime Location and Zoopla to 3% commission for full property management. For tenant finding with all the frills, such as hosted viewings and professional photos to check-in the total bill would be £445. This equates to less than half the commission charged by high-street agents. Another agent, Purplebricks.com is also very competitive. However, there can be drawbacks.

The main drawback is accessibility. If you have your contract with a local agent, they will be there when you want them. Online tends to be one step removed. You are strongly advised to consider what it is you want before entering into any deal with an online agent.

If you do appoint an agent to manage a property you should agree at the outset, in writing, exactly what constitutes management. Failure to understand the deal can cost you dearly. For example, in a lot of cases, an agent will charge you a fixed fee for finding a tenant, but will then exercise the right that they have given themselves in the initial contract to sign a new agreement and charge another months rent after the tenancy has expired. In this way they will charge you a months rent every six months for doing nothing at all.

Managing properties online

A free new letting platform enables buy-to-let landlords to manage their properties with the same tools as larger investors. Planetrent.co.uk takes you through every step of finding tenants, managing repairs and ensuring legal compliance. The company behind the platform is Ringley Group, which manages 12,000 homes for corporate investors. The platform's launch was brought forward by two months to help people to cope with social distancing. Pay-as-you-go extras include advertising on Rightmove and Zoopla (£60), digital contract signing (£20) and reference checks (£20).

What agents do

Agents will typically look after the following:

- Check tenants have the 'Right to Rent' Landlords must ensure tenants can legally reside in the UK before letting to them.
- The penalty for renting to someone without the right to rent is a £3,000 fine or even imprisonment.

- Give tenants a copy of the 'How to Rent' guide This guide lists landlord obligations and tenants' rights. You must either give tenants a hard copy or email it to them as an attachment. A link to the guide is not enough. Landlords who fail to do this are unable to evict tenants under a Section 21 Notice (Or 6A as appropriate).
- Tenants must be issued with a Gas Safety Certificate and an Energy performance certificate before they take up occupation. However, it is to be noted that In Trecarrell House Ltd v Rouncefield the Court of Appeal has held (by 2 to 1) that a landlord who has failed to provide his tenant with a gas safety certificate before the tenant enters into occupation is not prevented from using s.21, Housing Act 1988 to recover possession so long as he remedies that omission before service of the notice.
- Transfer the utility bills and the council tax into the name of the tenant. Sign agreements and take up references.
- Paying for repairs, although an agent will only normally do this if rent is being paid directly to them and they can make appropriate deductions.
- Chase rent arrears.
- Serve notices of intent to seek possession if the landlord instructs them to do so. An agent cannot commence court proceedings except through a solicitor.
- Visit the property at regular intervals and check that the tenants are not causing any damage.
- Deal with neighbour complaints.
- Banking rental receipts if the landlord is abroad

- Dealing with housing benefit departments if necessary. The extent to which agents actually do any or all of the above really depends on the caliber of the agent. It also depends on the type of agreement you have with the agent. Like your initial business plan, you should be very clear about what it is you want from the agent and how much they charge.

All buy-to-let landlords should consider taking out insurance for non-payment of rent. This is particularly important now in 2020, and beyond.

Beware! There are many so-called rental agencies, which have sprang up since the advent of "Buy to Let". These agents are not professional, do not know a thing about property management, are shady and should be avoided like the plague. Shop around and seek a reputable agent. A typical management fee might be 10-15 percent of the rent, although there is lots of competition and lower prices can be obtained.

As stated, there are many ways of charging and you should be clear about this. It is illegal for agencies to charge tenants for giving out a landlord's name and address. Most agencies will charge the landlord.

Advertisements

If you decide to dispense with the use of an agent, the classified advertisement section of local papers is a good place to seek potential tenants. Local papers are obviously cheaper than the nationals such as the Evening Standard in London or the broadsheets such as the Guardian. The type of newspaper you advertise in will largely reflect what type of customer you are looking for. An advert in the pages of the Times would indicate that you are looking for a well-heeled professional and this would be reflected in the type of property that you have to let. There are many free ad papers and also you may want to go to student halls of residence or hospitals in order to attract a potential tenant. When you do advertise, you should indicate clearly the type of property, in what area, what is required, i.e., male or female only, and the rent. You should try and avoid abbreviations as this causes confusion.

The public sector

One other source of income is the local authority or housing association. Quite often, your property will be taken off your hands under a five-year contract and you will receive a rental income paid direct for this period, with agreed increases. However, the local authority or housing association will demand a high standard before taking the property off your hands. Quite often the rent achieved will be lower than a comparable market rent, in return for full management and secure income.

If you wish to try this avenue then you should contact your local authority or nearest large association.

Company lets

Where the tenant is a company rather than an individual, the tenancy agreement will be similar to an assured shorthold but will not be bound by the six-month rule (see further on for details of assured shorthold tenancies). Company lets can be from any length of time, from a week to several years, or as long as you like.

The major difference between contracts and standard assured shorthold agreements is that the contract will be tailored to individual needs, and the agreement is bound by the provisions of contract law. Company tenancies are bound by the provisions of contract law and not by the Housing Acts. Note: if you are considering letting to a company you must use a letting agent or solicitor. Most companies will insist on it. The advantages of a landlord letting to a company are:

- A company or embassy has no security of tenure and therefore cannot be a sitting tenant.
- A company cannot seek to reduce the rent by statutory interventions.
- Rental payments are often made quarterly or six monthly in advance.
- The financial status of a company is usually more secure than that of an individual.
- Company tenants often require long-term lets to accommodate staff relocating on contracts of between one and five years.
- *The main disadvantages of company lets are:*
- A company tenancy can only be to a bona fide company or embassy, not to a private individual.
- A tenancy to a partnership would not count as a company let and may have some security of tenure.
- If the tenant is a foreign government, the diplomatic status of the occupant must be ascertained, as the courts cannot enforce breaches of contract with somebody who possesses diplomatic immunity.

- A tenancy to a foreign company not registered in the UK may prove time consuming and costly if it becomes necessary to pursue claims for unpaid rent or damage through foreign courts.

Short-lets

Although company lets can be of any length, it is becoming increasingly popular for companies to rent flats from private landlords on short-lets. A short-let is any let of less than six months. But here, it is essential to check the rules with any borough concerned.

Some boroughs will not allow lets for less than three months, as they do not want to encourage transient people in the neighborhood.

Generally speaking, short-lets are only applicable in large cities where there is a substantial shifting population. Business executives on temporary relocation, actors and others involved in television production or film work, contract workers and visiting academics are examples of people who might require a short-let.

From a landlord's point of view, short-lets are an excellent idea if you have to vacate your own home for seven or eight months, say, and do not want to leave it empty.

Short-let tenants provide useful extra income as well as keeping an eye on the place. Or if you are buying a new property and have not yet sold the old one, it can make good business sense to let it to a short-let tenant. Short-let tenants are, usually, from a landlord's point of view, excellent blue-chip occupants. They are busy professionals, high earners, out all day and used to high standards.

As the rent is paid by the company there is no worry for the landlord on this score either.

A major plus of short-lets is that they command between 20-50 percent more rent than the optimum market rent for that type of property. The one downside of short-lets is that no agency can guarantee permanent occupancy.

Student lets

Students usually come in groups and don't have many belongings, so they want houses or flats with lots of furnished bedrooms and large communal spaces. More than one toilet or bathroom would be a bonus that can help you charge higher rents.

Advantages of letting to students:

- Typically, students are not overly fussy about having state-of-the-art accommodation. For many it might be their first rental and they're more interested in being with their friends. Older properties with multiple rooms are ideal.
- You can charge rent per room. Since there are often more tenants in a student let than there would be family members in a similar property, especially if you have converted a living area into another bedroom, you can expect high returns.
- It is relatively easy to find tenants, particularly if you are close to a university campus!
- Students move on, so you are not tied into any long-term contracts.
- Generally, students are reliable tenants, easy-going and

undemanding. And best of all there's a new pool of them searching for accommodation every year.

Disadvantages of student lettings
- Demand for privately let student housing is being affected by the rise of purpose built private student accommodation. Research your area thoroughly.
- Bills for maintenance and repairs will probably be higher than usual but then you can offset this against the cost of not needing to provide expensive furniture and décor.
- You should always have a guarantor as students are coming from their family home.
- You may have a few months where your property is vacant during the summer holidays until the new term starts, but many student landlords successfully insist on 12-month leases.
- You might have to deal with noise complaints from neighbours or the local council if your tenants like to party.

While you are weighing up the advantages and disadvantages to student lettings, consider whether you will need to have certain accreditations as well. A property that is let to three or more tenants who are not related could be classed as a House in Multiple Occupation (HMO), in which case you will need to be licensed by your local authority.

You can also become an accredited landlord by a university, which means that you will be a recommended and trusted first port of call for students seeking new digs. Imagine how easy it would be to find tenants that way!

The DSS and housing benefit

Very few letting agencies or landlords will touch DSS or housing benefit tenants. However, as with student lets, there is another side of the coin. Quite often it is essential for a tenant on HB to have a guarantor, usually a homeowner, before signing a tenancy. Then it is up to the machinations of the benefit system to ensure that the landlord receives rent. The rent is assessed by a benefit officer, with the rent usually estimated at market price. There are rent levels set for each are that the benefit officer will not go above. A deposit is paid normally and rent can be paid direct to the landlord. This will require the tenant's consent No other conditions should be accepted by a private landlord. Rent certainly should not be paid direct to the tenant.

Although tenants on HB have a bad name, due to stereotyping, there are many reasons why a person may be on benefit and if housing benefit tenancies are managed well.

Holiday lets

Before the Housing Act 1988 became law, many landlords advertised their properties as holiday lets to bypass the then rules regarding security of tenure. Strictly speaking, a holiday let is a property let for no more than a month to any one tenant. If the same tenant renews for another month then the landlord is breaking the law.

Nowadays, holiday lets must be just that; let for a genuine holiday. If you have a flat or cottage that you wish to let for holiday purposes, whether or not you live in it yourself for part of the year, you are entering into a quite different agreement with the tenant.

Holiday lets are not covered by the Housing Act. The contract is finalised by exchange of letters with the tenant where they place a deposit and the owner confirms the booking. If the let is not for a genuine holiday you may have problems in evicting the tenant.

Generally speaking, certain services must be provided for the let to be deemed a holiday let. Cleaning services and changes of bed linen are essential. The amount paid by the holiday-maker will usually include utilities but would exclude use of the telephone, fax machine etc. If you have a property that you think is suitable for holiday let or wish to invest in one, there are numerous companies who will put you on to their books.

However, standards are high and there are a certain number of criteria to be met, such as safety checks, before they will consider taking you on. If possible, you should talk to someone with some experience of this type of let before entering into an agreement with an agency. The usual problems may arise, such as ensuring occupancy all year round and the maintenance of your property, which will be higher due to a high turnover. In addition to the above, the tax situation is changing for those with holiday lets which will mean the loss of certain allowances and the tightening up of others. This is discussed further in chapter 12, which deals with taxation issues.

Holiday lets-Letting through Airbnb or similar sites

Over the last few years, landlords have increasingly turned to companies like Airbnb to let their properties. However, what started out as a good concept has, as usual, been undermined by those looking for a quick return. .

A growing number of property owners are earning extra income by using short term let Companies such as Airsorted, GuestReady and Hostmaker have popped up in the past lew years and have reported phenomenal demand. They list customers properties on sites such as Booking.com, Airbnb and HomeAway and manage the booking process from start to finish. For example, Hostmaker, now manages more than 1,500 properties in eight European cities

These short term lettings agencies off a management service, which, for a fee, handle every aspect of each booking which also includes (if you pay for it) the changing of towels and sheets and just about everything to make sure that the property is ready for each short term guest. The management companies tend to operate in urban areas and typically levy a percentage fee.

Pass the Keys starts at 12% of rental income plus VAT. It operates in cities including Brighton, Bristol and Glasgow. Hostmaker operates in cities around the world such as London and Barcelona.

In the capital, it covers zonesl-2 plus locations such as Wimbledon and Golders Green. It charges 12%plusVAT-rising to 17% plus VAT for extras such as insurance and a personal account manager.

Guest ready. charges 12%.for a basic service or 20% for premium which includes insurance professional photography for the listing and 24/7 guest support. It operates in cities such as London. Edinburgh and Manchester. Airsorted covers locations including bath, Dublin, Cambridge and London.

Even when fees are taken into account, customers could earn more by using a service. However, if you are considering offering short-term lets check your mortgage. Properties specifically aimed at holiday letting will require a special mortgage. Most buy to let lenders will not allow holiday lets, usually requiring tenancies of at least six months. Lenders offering holiday let mortgages include Leeds, Market Harborough and Furness Building Societies. However, these mortgages typically preclude properties on a holiday site, as the lender will typically want to sell on the open market.

As short lets are classified as holiday lets, the owners of such lets can deduct interest payments from the rent before calculating their tax liability providing they can satisfy certain tests, including letting their property for at least 105 days a year. Buy-to-let investors can now offset only a portion of mortgage interest (falling to zero by 2020). Holiday-let owners can also claim the full cost of furnishing the property. For buy-to-let, it is repairs only.

Showing the property to the tenant

For traditional lettings, once you have found a tenant, the next stage is to make arrangements for viewing the property. It is a good idea to make all appointments on the same day in order to avoid wasting time. If you decide on a likely tenant, it is wise to take up references yourself if you are not using an agency who will do this for you. This will normally be a previous landlord's reference and also a bank reference plus a personal reference. Only when these have been received and you have established that the person(s) is/are safe should you go ahead. Make sure that no keys have been handed over until the cheque has been cleared and you are in receipt of a month's rent and a month's deposit.

Deposits-Tenancy Deposit Protection Scheme

The Tenancy Deposit Protection Scheme was introduced to protect all deposits paid to landlords after 6th April 2007. After this date, landlords and/or agents must use a government authorised scheme to protect deposits.

The need for such a scheme has arisen because of the historical problem with deposits. The scheme works as follows:

Moving into a property

At the beginning of a new tenancy agreement, the tenant will pay a deposit to the landlord or agent as usual. Within 30 days the landlord is required to give the tenant details of how the deposit is going to be protected including:

- the address of the rented property
- how much deposit you've paid
- how the deposit is protected
- the name and contact details of the tenancy deposit protection (TDP) scheme and its dispute resolution service
- their (or the letting agency's) name and contact details
- the name and contact details of any third party that's paid the deposit
- why they would keep some or all of the deposit
- how to apply to get the deposit back
- what to do if you can't get hold of the landlord at the end of the tenancy
- what to do if there's a dispute over the deposit

There are three tenancy deposit schemes that a landlord can opt for:

My Deposits
www.mydeposits.co.uk
info@mydeposits.co.uk
0333 321 9401
The Tenancy Deposit Scheme
www.tds.gb.com
0845 226 7837
The Deposit Protection Service
www.depositprotection.com
0330 303 0030

The schemes above fall into two categories, insurance based schemes and custodial schemes.

Custodial Scheme
- The tenant pays the deposit to the landlord
- The landlord pays the deposit into the scheme
- Within 14 days of receiving the deposit, the landlord must give the tenant prescribed information
- A the end of the tenancy, if the landlord and tenant have agreed how much of the deposit is to be returned, they will tell the scheme which returns the deposit, divided in the way agreed by the parties.
- If there is a dispute, the scheme will hold the disputed amount until the dispute resolution service or courts decide what is fair

- The interest accrued by deposits in the scheme will be used to pay for the running of the scheme and any surplus will be used to offer interest to the tenant, or landlord if the tenant isn't entitled to it.

Insurance based schemes

- The tenant pays the deposit to the landlord

- The landlord retains the deposit and pays a premium to the insurer (this is the key difference between the two schemes)
- Within 14 days of receiving a deposit the landlord must give the tenant prescribed information.
- At the end of the tenancy if the landlord and tenant agree how the deposit is to be divided or otherwise then the landlord will return the amount agreed
- If there is a dispute, the landlord must hand over the disputed amount to the scheme for safekeeping until the dispute is resolved. If for any reason the landlord fails to comply, the insurance arrangements will ensure the return of the deposit to the tenant if they are entitled to it.
- If a landlord or agent hasn't protected a deposit with one of the above then the tenant can apply to the local county court for an order for the landlord either to protect the deposit or repay it.

Rental guarantees

The landlord is always advised to obtain a guarantor if there is any potential uncertainty as to payment of rent. One example is where the tenant is on benefits. The guarantor will be expected to assume responsibility for the rent if the tenant ceases to pay at any time during the term of the tenancy.

****

Chapter 6

WHAT SHOULD BE PROVIDED UNDER THE TENANCY?

When you let a property, you have the choice of letting it furnished or unfurnished. There is a market for both but most properties will at least have white goods installed.

Furniture

A landlords decision whether or not to furnish property will depend on the sort of tenant that he is aiming to find. The actual legal distinction between a furnished property and an unfurnished property has faded into insignificance. If a landlord does let a property as furnished then the following would be the absolute minimum:

- Seating, such as a sofa and an armchair.
- Cabinet or sideboard.
- Kitchen tables and chairs.
- Cooker and refrigerator.
- Bedroom furniture.

Even unfurnished lets, however, are expected to come complete with a basic standard of furniture, particularly carpets and kitchen goods. If the landlord does supply electrical equipment then he or she will be responsible for carrying out annual checks along with annual checks on the boiler.

Services

Service charges, and the paying of these charges, will be the responsibility of the leaseholder. They will be included in the rent charged by the leaseholder to the tenant of the flat. However, the leaseholder should have some idea of the law in this area as it will be a cost which needs to be considered.

Usually, a landlord (freeholder) will only provide services to a tenant if the property is a flat situated in a block or house split into flats or is a house on a private estate. The services will include cyclical painting and maintenance, usually on a three to four year basis (flats) and gardening and cleaning plus repairs to the communal areas, plus communal electricity bills and water rates. These services should be outlined in the agreement and administered within a strict framework of law.

The 1985 Landlord and Tenant Act Section 18-30 as amended by the 1987 LTA and the 1996 Housing Act as amended by the 2002 Commonhold and Leasehold Reform Act are the main areas of law.

The landlord has rigid duties imposed within the Acts, such as the need to gain estimates before commencing works and also to consult with residents where the cost exceeds £250 per flat. The landlord must give the tenant 28 days notice of works to be carried out and a further 28 days to consider estimates, inviting feedback.

Tenants (leaseholders) have the right to see audited accounts and invoices relating to work. Service charges, as an extra payment over and above the rent are always contentious and it is an area that landlords need to be aware of.

Insurance

Strictly speaking, there is no legal duty on either landlord or tenant to insure the property. However, it is highly advisable for the landlord to provide buildings insurance as he/she stands to lose a lot more in the event of a disaster than the tenant. In addition, mortgagors will always want insurance in place to protect their own investment. A landlord letting property for a first time would be well advised to consult his/her insurance company before letting as there are different criteria to observe when a property is let and not to inform the company could invalidate the policy.

At the end of the tenancy

The tenancy agreement will normally spell out the obligations of the tenant at the end of the term. Essentially, the tenant will have an obligation to:

- Have kept the interior clean and tidy and in a good state of repair and decoration.
- Have not caused any damage.
- Have replaced anything that they have broken.
- Replace or pay for the repair of anything that they have damaged.
- Pay for the laundering of the linen.
- Pay for any other laundering and put anything that they have moved or removed back to how it was.

Sometimes a tenancy agreement will include for the tenants paying for anything that is soiled at their own expense, although sensible wear and tear is allowed for. The landlord will normally be able to recover any loss from the deposit that the tenant has given on entering the premises (see previous chapter for details of the Deposit Protection Schemes). However, sometimes, the tenants will withhold rent for the last month in order to recoup their deposit. The introduction of the Deposit Protection Schemes have made this more difficult in practice. It is up to the landlord to negotiate reimbursement for any damage caused, but this should be within reason. There is a remedy, which can be pursued in the small claims court if the tenants refuse to pay but this is rarely successful.

****

Chapter 7

UNDERSTANDING THE LAW

Explaining the law

As a landlord, or potential landlord, it is very important to understand the rights and obligations of both yourself and your tenant, exactly what can and what cannot be done once the tenancy agreement has been signed and the tenant has moved into the property.

In order to fully understand the law we should begin by looking at the main types of relationship between people and their homes.

The freehold and the lease

In law, there are two main types of ownership and occupation of property. These are: freehold and leasehold. These arrangements are very old indeed.

Freehold

If a person owns their property outright (usually with a mortgage) then they are a freeholder. The only claims to ownership over and above their own might be those of the building society or the bank, which lent them the money to buy the property. They will re-possess the property if the mortgage payments are not kept up with.

In certain situations though, the local authority (council) for an area can affect a person's right to do what they please with their home even if they are a freeholder. This will occur when planning powers are exercised, for example, in order to prevent the carrying out of alterations without consent. The local authority for your area has many powers and we will be referring to these regularly.

Leasehold

If a person lives in a property owned by someone else and has a written agreement allowing them to occupy the flat or house for a period of time i.e., giving them permission to live in that property, then they will, in the main, have a lease and either be a leaseholder or a tenant of a landlord. The main principle of a lease is that a person has been given permission by someone else to live in his or her property for a period of time. The person giving permission could be either the freeholder or another leaseholder. The tenancy agreement is one type of lease.

The position of the tenant

The tenant will usually have an agreement for a shorter period of time than the typical leaseholder. Whereas the leaseholder will, for example, have an agreement for ninety-nine years, the tenant will have an agreement, which either runs from week to week or month to month (periodic tenancy) or is for a fixed term, for example, six-months or one-year. These arrangements are the most common types of agreement between the private landlord and tenant.

The agreement itself will state whether it is a fixed term or periodic tenancy.

If an agreement has not been issued it will be assumed to be a fixed-term tenancy.

Both periodic and fixed term tenants will usually pay a sum of rent regularly to a landlord in return for permission to live in the property (more about rent and service charges later)

The tenancy agreement

The tenancy agreement is the usual arrangement under which one person will live in a property owned by another. Before a tenant moves into a property he/she will have to sign a tenancy agreement drawn up by a landlord or landlord's agent. *A tenancy agreement is a contract between landlord and tenant.* It is important to realize that when you sign a tenancy agreement, you have signed a contract with another person, which governs the way in which they will live in your property.

Different types of tenancy agreement
The protected tenancy - the meaning of the term

As a basic guide, if a person is a private tenant and signed their current agreement with a landlord before 15th January 1989 then they will, in most cases, be a protected tenant with all the rights relating to protection of tenure, which are considerable. Protection is provided under the 1977 Rent Act.

In practice, there are not many protected tenancies left and the tenant will usually be signing an assured shorthold tenancy.

The assured shorthold tenancy - what it means

If the tenant entered into an agreement with a landlord after 15th

January 1989 then they will, in most cases, be an assured tenant. We will discuss assured tenancies in more depth in chapter three.

In brief, there are various types of assured tenancy. The assured shorthold is usually a fixed term version of the assured tenancy and enables the landlord to recover their property after six months and to vary the rent after this time. *It is this tenancy that a private tenant will be signing.*

Other types of agreement

In addition to the above tenancy agreements, there are other types of agreement sometimes used in privately rented property. One of these is the company let, as we discussed in the last chapter, and another is the license agreement. The person signing such an agreement is called a licensee. Licenses will only apply in special circumstances where the licensee cannot be given sole occupation of his home and therefore can only stay for a short period with minimum rights.

What is inserted in the agreement?

Typically, any tenancy agreement will show:

- The name and address of the landlord and will state the names of the tenant(s). The type of tenancy agreement that is signed should be clearly indicated. In the main, in the private sector, the agreement between landlord and tenant will be an assured shorthold tenancy.
- Date of commencement of tenancy and rent payable. The date the tenancy began and the duration (fixed term or periodic) plus the amount of rent payable should be clearly shown.

- who is responsible for any other charges, such as water rates, council tax etc, and a description of the property you are renting out.

- In addition to the rent that must be paid there should be a clear indication of when a rent increase can be expected. This information is sometimes shown in other conditions of tenancy, which should be given to the tenant when they move into their home. The conditions of tenancy will set out landlords and tenants rights and obligations.

- Services provided under the tenancy and service of notice. If services are provided, i.e., if a service charge is payable, this should be indicated in the agreement. The tenancy agreement should indicate clearly the address to which notices on the landlord can be served by the tenant, for example, because of repair problems or notice of leaving the property. The landlord has a legal requirement to indicate this.

- Tenants obligations. The tenancy agreement will either be a basic document with the above information or will be more comprehensive. Either way, there will be a section beginning "the tenant agrees." Here the tenant will agree to move into the property, pay rent, use the property as an only home, not cause a nuisance to others, take responsibility for certain internal repairs, not sublet the property, i.e., create another tenancy, and various other things depending on the property.

- (The government is, at the moment, actively considering allowing tenants to sublet). It is important that when creating a tenancy agreement it complies with legislation.

- Landlords obligations. There should also be another section "the landlord agrees".
- Here, the landlord is contracting with the tenant to allow quiet enjoyment of the property.
- The landlord's repairing responsibilities are also usually outlined.
- Ending a tenancy. Finally, there should be a section entitled "ending the tenancy". This will outline the ways in which landlord and tenant can end the agreement. The landlord can only end a fixed term assured shorthold tenancy by issuing a s21 notice (so called because it arises out of section 21 of the Housing Act 1988, as amended) two months prior to the end of the tenancy. Many landlords issued this notice at the outset of the tenancy. However, the Deregulation Act 2015 has effectively stopped this practice and states that the landlord cannot now service the notice until the tenant has been in occupation for at least four months. The tenant, after the expiry of the fixed term, can give one months notice to leave. One more point worth noting is that, if the landlord issues notice, in the required format, by text or email this is likely to be accepted as valid notice.

The landlord must serve a notice by using Form 6A (replacing s21) for all tenancies created on or after October 1st 2015. This form must be used for all ASTs created on or after 1 October 2015 except for statutory periodic tenancies which have come into being on or after 1 October 2015 at the end of fixed term ASTs created before 1 October 2015.

See appendix for a sample tenancy and Form 6A. Also, take note of the governments temporary restrictions on serving notice following the coronavirus-six months notice must now be served when giving notice of intention to seek possession of a property-although it can be shorter for anti-social behavior (see below).

It is also in this section of the tenancy that the landlord should make reference to the "grounds for possession". Grounds for possession are circumstances where the landlord will apply to court for possession of his/her property.

Some of these grounds relate to what is in the tenancy, i.e., the responsibility to pay rent and to not cause a nuisance. Other grounds do not relate to the contents of the tenancy directly, but more to the law governing that particular tenancy. The grounds for possession are very important, as they are used in any court case brought against the tenant. Unfortunately, they are not always indicated in the tenancy agreement. The sample tenancy agreement in the appendix contains grounds for possession.

Recent government guidance in the light of the Coronavirus Act 2020.

'We strongly advise landlords not to commence or continue possession proceedings during this challenging time without a very good reason to do so. It is essential that we work together during these unprecedented times to keep each other safe'.

Under the Coronavirus Act 2020, most landlords will not be able to start possession proceedings unless they have given their tenants three-months' notice (now six months). This guidance reflects the modifications the Coronavirus Act makes to the notice requirements for seeking possession of their property under section 83 of the Housing Act 1985 and sections 8 and 21 of the Housing Act 1988. It sets out how landlords should give notice under those provisions and the forms they should use (See Section 81 and Schedule 29 of the Coronavirus Act 2020).

The responsibility of the landlord to provide a rent book

If the tenant is a weekly periodic tenant the landlord must provide him/her with a rent book and commits a criminal offence if he/she does not do so. This is outlined in the Landlord and Tenant Act 1985 sections 4 - 7. Under this Act any tenant can ask in writing the name and address of the landlord. The landlord must reply within twenty-one days of asking. As most tenancies nowadays are fixed term assured shortholds then it is not strictly necessary to provide a tenant with a rent book. *However, for the purposes of efficiency, and your own records, it is always useful to have a rent book and sign it each time rent is collected or a standing order is paid.*

Overcrowding

It is important to understand, when signing a tenancy agreement, that it is not permitted to allow the premises to become overcrowded, i.e., to allow more people than was originally intended, (which is outlined in the agreement) to live in the property. If a tenant does, then the landlord can take action to evict.

****

Chapter 8

RENT AND THE SOURCES OF TENANTS RENT

As must have become apparent by now, rent is the key to your survival as a residential landlord, It is vital to understand the issues surrounding rent and the payment of rent, in particular the various sources of rent, including housing benefit. At this point in time, with the effects of the coronavirus on peoples ability to pay rent, and the difficulty of evicting a tenant during the pandemic, (although this may or may not have passed by the time you read this book) attention to how and where rent comes from is very important.

Rent increases for assured shorthold tenants
The amount of rent a tenant must pay is set out in the tenancy agreement or agreed verbally with the tenant. Rent increases must follow certain rules. Landlords can charge a market rent for an assured shorthold tenancy.

Agreeing to pay a new rent
A landlord can increase the rent if the tenant agrees. It usually counts as agreeing to a new rent if the tenant pays a rent increase, even if they are unhappy about it.

Signing a new contract

If a tenant signs a new tenancy agreement, they have to pay the rent amount set out in the new agreement.

During a fixed-term tenancy

A landlord can't increase the rent during a fixed-term tenancy unless there is a rent review clause in the agreement that says the rent can be increased. Most assured shorthold tenancies start with a fixed term.

Rent increases when a rent review clause is used

A landlord can use a rent review clause in the tenancy agreement to increase the rent, if the contract contains one. A rent review clause usually sets out:

- when the increase will happen and how much notice the tenant will get
- how the rent can be increased (for example, a formula for calculating the new amount)
- Any rent review clause won't apply after the tenancy's fixed term ends, unless the tenancy continues as a contractual periodic tenancy. This happens if the tenancy agreement says something like: 'this contract is for a term of 12 months and thereafter from month to month'.

Rent increases using a section 13 notice

Section 13 (2) of the Housing Act 1988 provides for a landlord to increase rent in an assured shorthold tenancy agreement by issuing a Section 13 Notice.

If the rent is not stated in the tenancy agreement and the tenant does not agree to the proposed rent increase. (or if the rent review clause no longer applies). Your landlord must use Form 4 to give you valid notice. (see appendix). The section 13 procedure can only be used to increase the rent once a year. The tenant must get at least 1 month's notice of the increase if they have a weekly or monthly tenancy. They are entitled to more notice if the tenancy period is longer than a month. The landlord can serve the notice during the fixed term of the tenancy, but the rent increase can't take effect until after the fixed term has ended.

If the tenancy didn't start with a fixed term, a section 13 notice can't be used during the first year. If the tenant doesn't challenge the increase, the new rent applies after the notice expires.

Right to challenge a proposed section 13 increase

A tenant can apply to a tribunal for rent disputes to challenge a proposed section 13 rent increase. The tribunal must receive their application before the rent increase date given on the notice. They must continue to pay rent at the previously agreed rate until the tribunal makes its decision. The tribunal can decide that the tenant has accepted the rent increase if they pay it.

If the tribunal decides to increase the rent, the new rent usually applies from the rent increase date on the section 13 notice.

Negotiating the amount of an increase

It costs landlords time and money to re-let a property, so the tenant can try negotiating with the landlord if they :

- don't want to accept the rent increase at all

- would accept a lower rent increase
- want the increase to be rolled out in stages over a period of time

Council tax and the tenant

Council tax is based on properties, or dwellings, and not individual people. This means that there is one bill for each individual dwelling, rather than separate bills for each person. The number and type of people who live in the dwelling may affect the size of the final bill. A discount of 25 percent is given for people who live alone. Each property is placed in a valuation band with different properties paying more or less depending on their individual value.

Tenants who feel that their home has been placed in the wrong valuation band can appeal to their local authority council tax department.

Who has to pay the council tax?

In most cases the tenant occupying the dwelling will have to pay the council tax. That person is known as the 'liable person'. Nobody under the age of 18 can be a liable person. Couples living together will both be liable even if there is only one name appearing on the bill. However, a landlord will be responsible for paying the council tax where:

- there are several households living in one dwelling where households pay rent separately or;
- where people are under the age of 18;
- the people who live in the property are all asylum seekers who are not entitled to claim benefits including council tax benefits;

- the people who are staying in the property are there temporarily and have their main homes elsewhere; or
- the property is a care home, hospital, hostel or women's refuge.

Although the landlord has the responsibility for paying the council tax, he or she will normally try to pass on the increased cost through rents. However, there is a set procedure for a landlord to follow if he/she wishes to increase rent. The rules covering council tax liability can be obtained from a Citizens Advice Bureau or from your local authority council tax department.

****

Chapter 9

REPAIRS AND IMPROVEMENTS TO A PROPERTY- LANDLORDS AND TENANTS RESPONSIBILITY

Repairs and improvements generally: The landlord and tenants obligations

Repairs are essential works to keep the property in good order. Improvements and alterations to the property, e.g. the installation of a shower will enhance the property.

As we have seen, most tenancies are periodic, i.e. week-to-week or month-to-month. If a tenancy falls into this category, or is a fixed-term tenancy for less than seven years, and began after October 1961, then a landlord is legally responsible for most major repairs to the flat or house.

If a tenancy began after 15th January 1989 then, in addition to the above responsibility, the landlord is also responsible for repairs to common parts and service fittings.

The area of law dealing with the landlord and tenants repairing obligations is the 1985 Landlord and Tenant Act, section 11.

This section of the Act is known as a covenant and cannot be excluded by informal agreement between landlord and tenant. In other words the landlord is legally responsible whether he or she likes it or not. Parties to a tenancy, however, may make an application to a court mutually to vary or exclude this section.

Example of repairs a landlord is responsible for:
- Leaking roofs and guttering.
- Rotting windows.
- Rising damp.
- Damp walls.
- Faulty electrical wiring.
- Dangerous ceilings and staircases.
- Faulty gas and water pipes.
- Broken water heaters and boilers.
- Broken lavatories, sinks or baths.

In shared housing the landlord must see that shared halls, stairways, kitchens and bathrooms are maintained and kept clean and lit.

Normally, tenants are responsible only for minor repairs, e.g., broken door handles, cupboard doors, etc. Tenants will also be responsible for decorations unless they have been damaged as a result of the landlord's failure to do repair. A landlord will be responsible for repairs only if the repair has been reported. It is therefore important to keep a record of repairs in writing. If the repair is not carried out then action can be taken. Damages can also be claimed. Compensation can be claimed, with the appropriate amount being the reduction in the value of the premises to the tenant caused by the landlord's failure to repair. If the tenant carries out the repairs then the amount expended will represent the decrease in value. The tenant does not have the right to withhold rent because of a breach of repairing covenant by the landlord. However, depending on the repair, the landlord will not have a very strong case in court if rent is withheld.

Reporting repairs to landlords

The tenant has to tell the landlord or the person collecting the rent straight away when a repair needs doing.

It is advisable that it is in writing, listing the repairs that need to be done.

Once a tenant has reported a repair the landlord must do it within a reasonable period of time. What is reasonable will depend on the nature of the repair.

The tenants rights whilst repairs are being carried out

The landlord must ensure that the repairs are done in an orderly and efficient way with minimum inconvenience to the tenant. If the works are disruptive or if property or decorations are damaged the tenant can apply to the court for compensation or, if necessary, for an order to make the landlord behave reasonably. If the landlord genuinely needs the house empty to do the work he/she can ask the tenant to vacate it and can if necessary get a court order against the tenant. A written agreement should be drawn up making it clear that the tenant can move back in when the repairs are completed and stating what the arrangements for fuel charges and rent are.

Can the landlord put the rent up after doing repairs?

If there is a service charge for maintenance, the landlord may be able to pass on the cost of the work(s).

Tenants rights to make improvements to a property

Unlike carrying out repairs the tenant will not normally have the right to insist that the landlord make actual alterations to the home.

However, a tenant needs the following amenities and the law states that you should have:

- Bath or shower.
- Wash hand basin.
- Hot and cold water at each bath, basin or shower.
- An indoor toilet.

If these amenities do not exist then the tenant can contact the council's Environmental Health Officer. An improvement notice can be served on the landlord ordering him to put the amenity in.

Disabled tenants

If a tenant is disabled he/she may need special items of equipment in the accommodation. The local authority may help in providing and, occasionally, paying for these. The tenant will need to obtain the permission of the landlord. If you require more information then contact the social services department locally.

Gas safety

The Gas safety (Installation and use) Regulations 1998
The Gas Cooking Appliances (safety) Regulations 1989
Heating Appliances(Fireguard) (safety) Regulations 1991
Gas Appliances(Safety) Regulations 1995

All of the above are based on the fact that the supply of gas and the appliances in a dwelling are safe. A Gas Safety certificate is required to validate this.

Furniture Safety

Furniture and Furnishings (Fire) (Safety) Regulations 1988 and 1993 (as amended)

Landlords and lettings agents are included in these regulations. The regulations set high standards for fire resistance for domestic upholstered furniture and other products containing upholstery. The main provisions are:

- Upholstered articles (i.e. beds, sofas, armchairs etc) must have fire resistant filling material.
- Upholstered articles must have passed a match resistant test or, if of certain kinds (such as cotton or silk) be used with a fire resistant interliner.
- The combination of the cover fabric and the filling material must have passed a cigarette resistance test.

The landlord should inspect property for non-compliant items before letting and replace with compliant items.

Electrical Safety

Electrical Equipment (Safety) Regulations 1994
Plugs and Sockets etc. (Safety) Regulations 1994.
The Electrical Equipment Regulations came into force in January 1995. Both sets of regulations relate to the supply of electrical equipment designed with a working voltage of between 50 and 1000 volts ac. (or between 75 and 1000 volts dc.). The regulations cover all the mains voltage household electrical goods including cookers, kettles, toasters, electric blankets, washing machines, immersion heaters etc.

The regulations do not apply to items attached to land. This is generally considered to exclude the fixed wiring and built in appliances (e.g. central heating systems) from the regulations. Lettings agents and landlords should take the following action:

Essential:
Check all electrical appliances in all managed properties on a regular fixed term basis. Remove unsafe items and keep a record of checks.

Recommended:
- Have appliances checked by a qualified electrical engineer
- Avoid purchasing second hand electrical items
- There is no specific requirement for regular testing under the regulations. However, it is recommended that a schedule of checks, say on an annual basis, is put in place.

The availability of grants
There are a number of grants available to landlords at any one time. These will enable improvements to take place to a property. One of the main grants is the Disabled facilities Grant. However, there are more and your local authority can tell you what is available.

New regulations on Smoke and Carbon Monoxide detectors
From October 2015, all landlords, regardless of whether public or private sector, are required to install working smoke and carbon monoxide alarms in their properties, on each floor. The carbon monoxide alarms will need to be placed in high risk areas, i.e., where there are gas appliances.

Carbon monoxide detectors will not be required in properties where there are no gas or solid fuel appliances. A civil penalty of up to £5,000 will apply to landlords who fail to comply with this legislation.

Sanitation health and hygiene

Local authorities have a duty to serve an owner with a notice requiring the provision of a WC when a property has insufficient sanitation, sanitation meaning toilet waste disposal. They will also serve notice if it is thought that the existing sanitation is inadequate and is harmful to health or is a nuisance. Local authorities have similar powers under various Public Health Acts to require owners to put right bad drains and sewers, also food storage facilities and vermin, plus the containing of disease.

The Environmental Health Department, if it considers the problem bad enough will serve a notice requiring the landlord to put the defect right. In certain cases the local authority can actually do the work and require the landlord to pay for it. This is called work in default.

****

Chapter 10

MANAGING HOUSES IN MULTIPLE OCCUPATION

A house in multiple occupation – commonly known as an HMO – is a property which is rented by three or more tenants who aren't part of the same household (i.e. a family). Many landlords let HMOs as they consider them a more efficient way to run a rental portfolio. Although there may be more work to do, the opportunity to collect rent from a higher number of tenants and a potential higher rental yield is appealing. What's more, certain properties and locations are tailor-made for HMOs. For example, a busy student area with large, extendable properties. When it comes to tenants, HMOs are sometimes preferable due to potentially lower rent payments and the opportunity to live with more people.

As landlords have had to deal with increased regulation and financial setbacks in recent years, such as Section 24 and the 3% stamp duty surcharge, many have looked for ways to maximise the potential of their portfolios. Alongside incorporation, one of the most popular strategies has been to convert rental properties into HMOs in order to benefit from higher yields and rental returns.

Converting a property into an HMO

If you're considering converting a property into an HMO, there are several things you'll need to do, from meeting legal requirements to making the property habitable for more people.

What are the first steps?

HMO Licensing

One of the most important legal aspects of letting an HMO is getting the relevant licence in place. The rules surrounding HMO licensing were updated in October 2018 and were expected to affect up to 177,000 additional properties at the time.

If you're letting an HMO, it's highly likely you'll need some sort of licence. If your property is let to five or more tenants from more than one household, some or all of the tenants share toilet, bathroom or kitchen facilities and at least one tenant pays rent, then your property will be considered as a large HMO and will need a licence. If some, but not all, of these criteria apply, then you may still need a licence and it's wise to check with your local authority. HMO licences are valid for five years at a time and you'll require a separate licence for each HMO you're running.

HMO Fire Safety & Smoke alarms

As well as applying for a licence, there are various other compliance measures you'll need to meet. These include sending a valid gas safety certificate to your local authority each year, installing the relevant smoke alarms and carbon monoxide detectors and having safety certificates for electrical appliances available on request.

HMO Minimum Room Sizes

At the same time as the licensing changes, guidelines for minimum HMO room sizes were also introduced with landlords needing to adhere to the following guidelines:

- Obligation to notify the local housing authority of any room in the HMO with a floor area of less than 4.64 square metres and ensure that the floor area of any room in the HMO used as sleeping accommodation by one person aged over 10 years is not less than 6.51 square metres.
- Ensure that the floor area of any room in the HMO used as sleeping accommodation by two persons aged over 10 years is not less than 10.22 square metres.
- Ensure that the floor area of any room in the HMO used as sleeping accommodation by one person aged under 10 years is not less than 4.64 square metres.
- Ensure that any room in the HMO with a floor area of less than 4.64 square metres is not used as sleeping accommodation.
- As part of these regulations, there were also new rules on overcrowding for landlords to comply with:
- Where any room in the HMO is used as sleeping accommodation by persons aged over 10 years only, it is not used as such by more than the maximum number of persons aged over 10 years specified in the licence.
- Where any room in the HMO is used as sleeping accommodation by persons aged under 10 years only, it is not used as such by more than the maximum number of persons aged under 10 years specified in the licence.
- Where any room in the HMO is used as sleeping accommodation by persons aged over 10 years and persons aged under 10 years, it is not used as such by more than the maximum number of persons aged over 10 years specified in

the licence. Depending on your local authority, there may be other criteria for you to meet in order to let a compliant HMO.

Does your property need converting to a HMO?

If your property is not HMO-ready, you may need to make some adjustments to make it suitable for three or more tenants from separate households. Always remember the HMO property needs to be habitable and provide enough space for tenants to live comfortably. As well as your compliance obligations outlined above, the key things you'll need to consider are space, layout, facilities, furniture and appliances.

If you convert your property into an HMO, it will be visited by your local authority within five years. They will carry out a Housing Health and Safety Rating System (HHSRS) risk assessment to identify any issues. It's worth noting, however, that the HHSRS was reviewed by the Government in 2019 and therefore its guidelines could be updated in the future.

If any unacceptable risks – such as asbestos, carbon monoxide or radiation - are found during the assessment, you will need to address them immediately.

HMO Room conversions

It's likely you'll be converting the use of some rooms. For example, spare rooms may be converted to additional bathrooms and reception rooms to additional bedrooms. You may also need to move or construct walls in order to alter room sizes - these are all aspects you'll need to plan carefully before undertaking any work.

It's also advisable to use a professional when working on the more significant parts of the conversion and determine whether you need planning permission for any major renovations.

Converting the garage into additional living space is another popular conversion option for HMO landlords. The likelihood is this will need planning permission, so again you'll need to check with your local council before undertaking any work. In many cases, traditional Victorian terraced houses and similar properties are ideal for HMO conversion. This is due to their spaciousness and the size of the reception rooms.

For example, in a three-bedroom terraced house a landlord could convert one reception room and the loft into bedrooms to turn it into a five-bedroom HMO. Converting reception rooms is often essential, but not always the right decision. In the perfect scenario, the property will have two reception rooms - one of which can be converted, leaving the other room to remain as a dining or living space. Some renters might be put off properties with no living room or reception space, so it's something you'll need to consider carefully. Depending on the property, converting it into an HMO is going to be expensive and take some time. You need to make sure you budget properly and don't expect instant financial returns. Five quick HMO renovation tips

- Remember your outdoor space - You may be tempted to focus on the interior of the property, but any outdoor space is equally important if you want your HMO to appeal to long-term tenants who are looking for a home. Seating and BBQ areas are likely to be popular with the modern renter.

- Prioritise kitchens and bathrooms - These enduringly popular rooms could be the dealbreaker when it comes to renters choosing your property. Tenants' expectations are likely to be high, so make sure you furnish to a high standard and add some nice touches such as an electric towel rail.
- Don't skimp on important features - while you'll want to keep costs down as much as possible, there is no point on being cheap when it comes to important features such as fridges, ovens, sofas and beds. This approach will only end up costing you more in the long-term.
- Maximise your space - If you've got tenants from three or more separate households in your property, you need to make it as spacious as possible. There are plenty of interior design tricks and tips out there to help you make the home feel more spacious without huge material changes.
- Be 100% ready to let - Tenants don't want to be moving into a building site and it's important you have everything finished before they move in to reduce the chances of damage or problems early in the tenancy.

HMO safety requirements

While converting your property to make it suitable for multiple tenants to live in, there are also a range of additional safety requirements you'll need to follow in order to let a compliant HMO. Fire safety will be one of your principle considerations. You will need to install smoke alarms, keep them in working order and be able to provide your local authority with a declaration of their safe condition on request.

Alongside this, as with all lets, you'll need to ensure that all gas appliances are maintained, with a Gas Safe registered engineer carrying out a gas safety check each year. All electrical installations and appliances you provide will need to be safe to use, while any furniture and furnishing you provide must meet the fire resistance regulations. Meanwhile, you will need an Electrical Installation Condition Report (EICR) and test certificates for your electrical appliances. It's likely you'll also need to install fire doors in certain places - make sure that your tenants know not to obstruct them or prop them open.

What's more, you'll need to keep all exits clear from obstructions (and advise tenants to do so too), while marking fire exits and providing tenants with instructions on what to do in the event of a fire. Some other safety requirements you'll need to consider when preparing your HMO to let could include:

- Locks for each bedroom (preferably thumb turn locks)
- Emergency lighting for fire safety
- Keeping pest control treatment records

The safety requirements for HMOs are very extensive and are likely to differ depending on your local authority. Therefore, it's always best to check with them first to get a full list of safety requirements before embarking on your conversion plans.

Fitness for human habitation
Another piece of legislation landlords need to comply with - including those letting HMOs - is the Homes (Fitness for Human Habitation) Act 2018, which came into force in March 2019.

The legislation means all rented accommodation must be suitable for human habitation at the start of the tenancy and throughout. It also provides tenants with greater powers to hold their landlord to account if their property is substandard. To ensure your property is fit for human habitation, there are a range of potential issues you'll need to avoid. Some of these include:

- damp
- ventilation
- overcrowding
- drainage
- water supply

What's more, if the property contains any of the 29 hazards outlined in the HHSRS regulations, it's likely to be deemed unfit for human habitation by the courts. As a landlord, you'll be exempt from 'acts of God' and any issues caused by tenants.

Tenant turnover

One of the key differences between an HMO and a standard rental property is that you could encounter a higher turnover of tenants. Therefore, it's advisable to put aside at least two months' worth of rent each year to cover potential void periods.

You'll also need to make sure you have all the right tenancy documentation in place and an efficient referencing process for new tenants.

Property damage

Another crucial factor to remember is that, due to the nature of having more tenants, the property is likely to come under more stress over the course of a tenancy.

Bathrooms, kitchens, floors and doors will all take a lot more wear and so you need to make sure you're ready for this and are prepared to respond to all reasonable repair requests with speed and efficiency – as with any other tenancy.

Be sure to check that your landlord insurance policy, if you have one, is suitable for a HMO – as not all landlord insurance policies cover a house of multiple occupancy.

Buy-to-let mortgage terms for HMOs
When preparing to let an HMO, you'll need to check your buy-to-let mortgage terms. Not all agreements allow properties to be let as HMOs, so check your terms and conditions.

If you're not sure about something, you can check-in with your lender or speak to a buy-to-let mortgage broker. Your agreement may allow you to get started right away or you may need to arrange a different type of mortgage to proceed.

Research and budgeting
As mentioned above, you'll need to prepare the property fully before letting it, taking no shortcuts and making sure you have enough money put aside to cover maintenance costs during and after the tenancy.

Converting a rental property to an HMO can be an effective investment with highly profitable rental yields, but it does require more work and upkeep.

Therefore, before jumping straight in, you'll need to do your research, take your time and carefully compare the additional work and expense against the additional profit you're likely to make.

As with all projects of this nature, a considered combination of research and budgeting can help you to make the right decisions and ultimately benefit from the greater yields on offer from HMO properties.

****

Chapter 11

RECOVERING A PROPERTY AFTER THE TENANCY ENDS OR BEFORE THE TENANCY ENDS

Fast-track possession

When reading this chapter, please take note of the temporary changes introduced by The Coronavirus Act 2020, as outlined in the introduction, mainly restrictions on serving notices and delayed repossession hearings.

Previously, a landlord will have served a section 21 notice on the tenant at the start of the tenancy. However, following the passage of the Deregulation Act 2015, the landlord can no longer do this and must serve the notice after the tenant has been in occupation for four months. This brings the tenancy to an end on the day of expiry, i.e. on the day of expiry of the six month period, or 12 month period, whichever is appropriate. It should be noted that if a landlord takes a deposit from the tenant then every deposit must be registered with the appropriate deposit service before the landlord can serve the s21 notice.

For all AST's issued after October 1st 2015, a Form 6a is served (see appendix).

On expiry of the notice, if it is the landlord's intention to take possession of the property then the tenants should leave. It is worthwhile writing a letter to the tenants one month before expiry reminding them that they should leave. In the event of the tenant refusing to leave, then the landlord has to then follow a process termed 'fast track possession'.

This entails filling in the appropriate forms (N5B) which can be accessed from: www.gov.uk/accelerated-possession-eviction. the process is online and costs £355 (2020/2021)

Assuming that a valid form 6 notice has been served on the tenant, the accelerated possession proceedings can begin and the forms completed online which are then lodged with the court dealing with the area where the property is situated. In order to grant the accelerated possession order the court will require the following:

- The assured shorthold agreement
- The section 21 notice (or form 6a notice)
- Evidence of service of the notice

The best form of service of the notice is by hand. If the notice has already served then evidence that the tenant has received it will be required. A copy must also be served on the tenant. This will be done by the court although it might help if the landlord also serves a copy informing the tenant that they are taking proceedings. If the tenant disputes the possession proceedings in any way they will have 14 days to reply to the court. If the case is well founded and the paperwork is in order then there should be no case for defence. Note that In Trecarrell House Ltd v Rouncefield the Court of Appeal has held (by 2 to 1) that a landlord who has failed to provide his tenant with a gas safety certificate before the tenant enters into occupation is not prevented from using s.21, Housing Act 1988 to recover possession so long as he remedies that omission before service of the notice.

Once the accelerated possession order has been granted then this will need to be served on the tenant, giving them 14 days to vacate. In certain circumstances, if the tenant pleads hardship the court can grant extra time to leave, six weeks as opposed to two weeks. If they still do not vacate then an application will need to be made to court for a bailiffs warrant to evict the tenants. An accelerated possession order remains in force for six years from the date it was granted.

Going to court to end the tenancy

Taking into account the aforementioned restrictions imposed by the Coronavirus Act 2020, there may come a time when the landlord needs to go to court to regain possession of a property. This will usually arise when the contract has been breached by the tenant, for non-payment of rent or for some other breach such as nuisance or harassment. As we have seen, a tenancy can be brought to an end in a court on one of the grounds for possession. However, as the tenancy will usually be an assured shorthold then it is necessary to consider whether the landlord is in a position to give two months notice and withhold the deposit, as opposed to going to court. The act of withholding the deposit will entail the landlord refusing to authorize the payment to the tenant online. This then brings arbitration into the frame. Deposit schemes have an arbitration system as an integral part of the scheme.

If the landlord decides, for whatever reason, to go to court, then any move to regain the property for breach of agreement will commence in the county court in the area in which the property is. The first steps in ending the tenancy will necessitate the serving of a notice of seeking possession using one of the Grounds for Possession detailed earlier in the book. If the tenancy is protected then 28 days must be given, the notice must be in prescribed form and served on the tenant personally (preferably).

If the tenancy is an assured shorthold, which is more often the case now, then 14 days notice of seeking possession can be used. In all cases the ground to be relied upon must be clearly outlined in the notice.

If the case is more complex, then this will entail a particulars of claim being prepared, usually by a solicitor, as opposed to a standard possession form.

A fee is paid when sending the particulars to court, which should be checked with the local county court. The standard form which the landlord uses for routine rent arrears cases is called the N119 and the accompanying summons is called the N5. Both of these forms can be obtained from the court or from :

justice.gov.uk/HMCTS/FormFinder.do

When completed, the forms should be sent in duplicate to the county court and a copy retained for the landlord. The court will send a copy of the particulars of claim and the summons to the tenant. They will send the landlord a form which gives him a case number and court date to appear, known as the return date.

On the return date, the landlord will arrive at court at least 15 minutes early. He can represent yourself in simple cases but will be advised to use a solicitor for more contentious cases.

If the tenant is present then they will have a chance to defend themselves. A number of orders are available. However, if a landlord has gone to court on the mandatory ground eight then if the fact is proved then they will get possession immediately.

If not, then the judge can grant an order, suspended whilst the tenant finds time to pay. In a lot of cases, it is more expedient for a landlord to serve notice-requiring possession, if the tenancy has reached the end of the period, and then wait two months before the property is regained. This saves the cost and time of going to court particularly if the ground is one of nuisance or other, which will involve solicitors.

If the landlord regains possession of A property midway through the contractual term then he will have to complete the possession process by use of bailiff, pay a fee and fill in another form, Warrant for Possession of Land.

For further detailed information on repossessing a property you should go to:

https://www.gov.uk/evicting-tenants/possession-hearings-and-orders

****

Chapter 12

PRIVATE TENANCIES IN SCOTLAND

The law governing the relationship between private landlords and tenants in Scotland is different to that in England. Since the beginning of 1989, new private sector tenancies in Scotland were covered by the Housing (Scotland) Act 1988. Following the passage of this Act, private sector tenants no longer had any protection as far as rent levels were concerned and tenants enjoyed less security of tenure. However, **The Private Housing (Tenancies) (Scotland) Act 2016**, passed by the Scottish Parliament and coming into force on 1st December 2017 has changed the law concerning private tenancies in Scotland. The main provisions of the Act are outlined below.

The Private Residential Tenancy

On 1 December 2017 a new type of tenancy came into force, called the private residential tenancy, it replaced assured and short assured tenancy agreements for all new tenancies from 1st December 2017. as a result of passing of The Private Housing (Tenancies) (Scotland) Act 2016. The new Scottish Private Residential Tenancy, (SPRT) delivers improved security of tenure for tenants, including students in smaller purpose built and mainstream private rented accommodation, and also the power for local authorities to designate rent pressure zones within their jurisdiction. There is also a streamlined procedures for starting and ending a tenancy and a model agreement for landlords and tenants.

The SPRT is the standard tenancy agreement between residential landlords and tenants and replaced the most common types of residential tenancies in Scotland – the Short Assured Tenancy and the Assured Tenancy.

What changes has the private residential tenancy brought in?

Any tenancy that started on or after 1 December 2017 will be a private residential tenancy. These new tenancies will bring in changes and improvements to the private rented sector, including:

- **No more fixed terms** - private residential tenancies are open ended, meaning a landlord can't ask a tenant to leave just because they have been in the property for 6 months as they can with a short assured tenancy.
- **Rent increases** – a tenant's rent can only be increased once every 12 months (with 3 months notice) and if they think the proposed increase is unfair they can refer it to a rent officer.
- **Longer notice period** - if a tenant has lived in a property for longer than 6 months the landlord will have to give them at least 84 days notice to leave (unless they have broken a term in the tenancy).
- **Simpler notices** - the notice to quit process has been scrapped and replaced by a simpler notice to leave process.
- **Model tenancy agreement** - the Scottish Government have published a model private residential tenancy that can be used by landlords.

Person already an assured/short assured tenant

If a tenant was already renting and were an assured or short assured tenant, on 1 December 2017, their tenancy will continue as normal until they or their landlord brings it to an end following the correct procedure.

If a landlord then offers a tenant a new tenancy this will be a private residential tenancy.

What is a private residential tenancy?

A private residential tenancy is one that meets the following conditions:

- the tenancy started on or after 1 December 2017
- it is let to a person as a separate dwelling (home)
- the person must be an individual, meaning not a company
- it's their main or only home
- they must have a lease (although a written agreement not needed for a lease to exist)
- the tenancy is not a exemptions tenancy, as listed below.

Tenancy agreements

A person have the right to a tenancy agreement, which can be either a written or electronic copy, within 28 days of the start of the tenancy. The Scottish Government has published a model tenancy that a landlord can use to set up a tenancy. This tenancy plus a set of notes that a landlord must give to the tenant can be accessed at www.mygov.scot/tenancy-agreement-scotland.

This tenancy agreement contains certain statutory terms that outline both parties rights and obligations including:

- The tenant's and landlord/letting agent's contact details
- The address and details of the rented property
- The start date of the tenancy
- How much the rent is and how it can be increased
- How much the deposit is and information about how it will be registered
- Who is responsible for insuring the property.
- The tenant has to inform the landlord when they are going to be absent from the property for more than 14 days
- The tenant will take reasonable care of the property
- The condition that the landlord must make sure the property is in, including the repairing standard.
- That the tenant must inform the landlord the need of any repairs.
- That the tenant will give reasonable access to the property, when the landlord has given at least 48 hours notice
- The process that the tenancy can be brought to an end

If a landlord uses the Scottish Government's' model tenancy they should also give the tenant the 'Easy Read Notes' which will explain the tenancy terms in plain English. If a landlord does not use the model tenancy they must give the tenant the private residential tenancy statutory terms: supporting notes, with their lease, which will explains the basic set of terms that a landlord has to include in the lease.

Rent Increases

The rent can only be increase once every 12 months and the landlord needs to give a tenant 3 months notice, using the correct notice of the rent increase. If the tenant doesn't agree to the rent increase they can refer it to the local rent officer. The referral to the rent officer must be done within 21 days of receiving the rent increase notice.

When a referral is made to the rent officer, they will first issue a provisional order which will suggest the amount the rent can be increased. The tenant will have 14 days from the date the provisional order is issued to request a reconsideration. If the tenant requests a reconsideration the rent officer will look at it again before making a final order and telling them the date that the increase will take place.

Ending a tenancy

If a tenant wants to end the tenancy, then they will have to give the landlord 28 days notice in writing. The notice has to state the day on which the tenancy is to end, normally the day after notice period has expired. The tenant can agree a different notice period with the landlord as long it is in writing. If there is no agreed notice then 28 days notice is the minimum required.

Landlord access

The tenant has to allow reasonable access to the landlord to carry out repairs, inspections, or valuations when the landlord has given at least 48 hours' written notice, or access is required urgently for the landlord to view or carry out works in relation to the repairing standard.

If a tenant refuses access the landlord can make an application to the First Tier Tribunal Housing and Property Chamber who may make an order allowing them access.

Getting repairs carried out

As with other tenancies, the landlord has to keep the property wind and watertight, and in a condition that is safe to live in. The landlord is also responsible for making sure that the property repairing standard is met.

This is a basic level of repair that is required by law. The landlord must give the tenant information on the repairing standard and what they can do if the property does not meet it.

If a tenant wants to carry out work on their home, such as redecorating or installing a second phone line, they will need to seek permission from the landlord. Some tenancy agreements will include a clause telling the tenant whether they can carry out this kind of work.

Can a tenant sublet or pass their tenancy on to someone else?

A tenant cannot sublet, take in a lodger or pass their tenancy on to someone else before first getting written agreement from the landlord.

Tenancies that cannot be private residential tenancy

Almost all new private tenancies created on or after 1st December 2017 will be private residential tenancies. However, there are a number of exemptions, including the following:

- Tenancies at a low rent

- Tenancies of shops
- Licensed premises
- Tenancies of agricultural land
- Lettings to students (meaning purpose built student accommodation)
- Holiday lettings
- Resident landlords
- Police Housing
- Military Housing
- Social Housing
- Sublet, assigned etc. social housing
- Homeless persons
- Persons on probation or released from prison etc.
- Accommodation for asylum seekers
- Displaced persons
- Shared ownership
- Tenancies under previous legislation
- Assured or short assured tenancies

Short assured and assured tenancies

Most residential lettings in Scotland made after 2 January 1989 and before 1st December 2017 are short assured tenancies. Those that aren't short assured are normally assured tenancies.

Short assured tenancies

This was the most common type of tenancy. A short assured tenancy makes it easier for a landlord to repossess a property than an assured tenancy.

Before any agreement is signed, a landlord must use form AT5 to tell new tenants that the tenancy will be a short assured tenancy. (see appendix). If they don't, the tenancy will automatically be an assured tenancy.

Initially, a short assured tenancy must be for 6 months or more. After the first 6 months, the tenancy can be renewed for a shorter period.

Assured tenancies

At the beginning of an assured tenancy, it will be classed as a 'contractual assured tenancy' for a fixed period of time. The tenancy automatically becomes a 'statutory assured tenancy' if:

- the landlord ends the tenancy by issuing a notice to quit (eg because they want to change the agreement) and the tenant stays in the property
- the fixed period covered by the tenancy comes to an end and the tenant stays in the property

There are different rights and responsibilities on both landlord and tenant depending on the type of assured tenancy.

What the landlord must include in a tenancy agreement

If a landlord used an assured or short assured tenancy, the agreement must be written down.

It must include:

- the names of all people involved
- the rental price and how it's paid

- the deposit amount and how it will be protected (see below)
- when the deposit can be fully or partly withheld (eg to repair damage caused by tenants)
- the property address
- the start and end date of the tenancy
- any tenant or landlord obligations
- who's responsible for minor repairs
- which bills your tenants are responsible for
- a statement telling the tenant that antisocial behaviour is a breach of the agreement

For other types of tenancy, it's still good practice to put the agreement in writing. including other information. To avoid any confusion later, the landlord can include other information in the agreement, such as:

- whether the tenancy can be ended early and how this can be done
- information on how and when the rent will be reviewed
- whether the property can be let to someone else (sublet) or have lodgers

Changes to tenancy agreements
The landlord must get the agreement of their tenants if they want to make changes to the terms of their tenancy agreement.

Preventing discrimination
Unless the landlord have a very strong reason, they must change anything in a tenancy agreement that might discriminate against tenants on the grounds of:

- gender
- sexual orientation
- disability (or because of something connected with their disability)
- religion or belief
- being a transsexual person
- the tenant being pregnant or having a baby

Ending a Short assured tenancy

To get a property back, the landlord must give tenants a 'notice to quit' and a 'Section 33 notice'. For a short assured tenancy, the minimum notice period is 40 days if the tenancy is for 6 months or longer. For a tenancy that is continuing on a month by month basis after the original period has ended, the notice period is a minimum of 28 days. The landlord must give 2 months notice when giving a Section 33 notice. They can issue both the notice to quit and Section 33 notice at the same time. (see appendix)

Ending a tenancy early

A landlord can end a tenancy early if the tenant breaks a condition of the tenancy agreement orlandlord and tenant agree to end the tenancy

If tenants don't leave

If the notice period expires and tenants don't leave the property, the landlord can start the process of eviction through the courts. A landlord must tell tenants of their intention to get a court order by giving them a 'notice of intention to raise proceedings' (AT6) (see appendix).

If tenants want to leave

The tenancy agreement should say how much notice tenants need to give before they can leave the property. If the notice isn't mentioned in the tenancy agreement, the minimum notice a tenant can give is:

- 28 days if their tenancy runs on a month-to-month basis (or if it's for less than a month)
- 40 days if their tenancy is for longer than 3 months

Houses in multiple occupation (HMOs)

If a tenant is living in a bedsit, shared flat, lodging, shared house, hostel or bed and breakfast accommodation it's likely that they will be living in a house in multiple occupation. A landlord will have an HMO if:

- tenants live with two or more other people, and
- they don't belong to the same family, and
- they share some facilities, e.g. a bathroom or kitchen, and
- the accommodation is their only or main home (if they are a student, their term-time residence counts as their main home).

If they live with a homeowner their family doesnt count as 'qualifying persons' when deciding whether or not a property is an HMO.

So for example, if they share accommodation with the owner and one other unrelated lodger, they won't live in an HMO. If they live with the owner and two other unrelated lodgers, they will live in an HMO.

Before the council gives a landlord an HMO licence, it will carry out the following checks:

Does the property meet the required standards?
To meet the standards expected of an HMO property:

- the rooms must be a decent size, for example, every bedroom should be able to accommodate a bed, a wardrobe and a chest of drawers.
- there must be enough kitchen and bathroom facilities for the number of people living in the property, with adequate hot and cold water supplies.
- adequate fire safety measures must be installed, for example the landlord must provide smoke alarms and self-closing fire doors.
- make sure there is an emergency escape route.
- all gas and electrical appliances must be safe.
- heating, lighting and ventilation must all be adequate.
- the property should be secure, with good locks on the doors and windows.
- There must be a phone line installed so that tenants can set up a contract with a phone company to supply the service.

In order to keep their HMO licence, a landlord must maintain the property properly:

- **Common parts** - these must be kept clean and in good repair (for example, the stairwell, hall, shared kitchen and bathroom). However, the landlord can include a clause in the tenancy agreement which passes this responsibility onto the tenants.

- **Shared facilities** - these should be kept in good repair (for example, the cooker, boiler, fridge, sinks, bath and lighting)
- **Heating, hot water and ventilation** - these facilities must all be kept in good order
- **Gas safety** - all gas appliances and installations must be safe (for example, a gas fire, boiler or cooker) - these should be checked once a year by a Gas Safe Register engineer
- **Electrical safety** - all electrical appliances and installations must be safe - these should be tested every three years by a contractor approved by the National Inspection Council for Electrical Installation Contracting (NICEIC) or SELECT, Scotland's trade association for the electrical, electronics and communications systems industry
- **Fire precautions** - all fire precautions (for example, smoke alarms and fire extinguishers) must be in good working order and that the fire escape route is kept safe and free from obstructions
- **Furniture** - all furniture supplied must meet safety standards (for example, isn't flammable)
- **Roof, windows and exterior** - these must all be adequately maintained
- **Rubbish** - enough rubbish bins must be provided
- **Deposits** - tenants deposits must be returned within a reasonable time when they move out, preferably within 14 days.

The landlord should also put up notices in the accommodation:
- giving the name and address of the person responsible for managing it so that the tenant can contact them whenever necessary
- explaining what the tenant should do in an emergency, for example if there is a gas leak or a fire.

- **Tenants responsibilities:**
- **Repairs** – the tenant should let the landlord know if anything in the property needs repairing, particularly if this is something they are responsible for keeping in good order, such as the roof, boiler or toilet
- **Damage** – the tenant must take good care of the property and try not to damage anything
- **Rubbish** - not let rubbish pile up in or around the property but dispose of it properly in the bins provided
- **Inspections** - let the landlord inspect the property so they can check whether any maintenance work needs doing. Normally this should happen once every six months.
- The landlord must give 24 hours' written notice before coming round.
- **Behave responsibly** - make sure that the tenant doesnt behave in a way that can annoy or upset neighbours. The landlord is responsible for dealing with any complaints made by neighbours and must take action if they are unhappy with tenants behaviour.

Safeguarding Tenancy Deposits

A tenancy deposit scheme is a scheme provided by an independent third party to protect deposits until they are due to be repaid. Three schemes are now operating:

- Letting Protection Service Scotland
- Safedeposits Scotland
- Mydeposits Scotland

Landlord's legal duties

The legal duties on landlords who receive a tenancy deposit are:

- to pay deposits to an approved tenancy deposit scheme
- to provide the tenant with key information about the tenancy and deposit

Information about the schemes

Further details about the individual schemes are available on the individual scheme web sites below. Email addresses and telephone numbers are also included. All three schemes have a range of information available for both landlords (and their agents) as well as tenants and these include how landlords can join the schemes, how to submit deposits, how to ask for repayment of deposits and how the dispute resolution service will work.

Letting Protection Service Scotland

www.lettingprotectionscotland.com
Address:
The Pavilions
Bridgwater Road
Bristol BS99 6BN

Email contact: events@lettingprotectionscotland.com
Telephone: 0330 303 0031

SafeDeposits Scotland

www.safedepositsscotland.com

Address:

Lower Ground

250 West George Street

Glasgow

G2 4QY

Email contact: info@safedepositsscotland.com

Telephone: 03333 213 136

Mydeposits Scotland

www.mydepositsscotland.co.uk

Address:

Premiere House

Elstree Way

Borehamwood

Hertfordshire

WD6 1JH

 Email contact: info@mydepositsscotland.co.uk

Telephone: 0333 321 9402

****

Chapter 13

INCOME TAX AND OTHER ISSUES WITH BUY TO LET PROPERTY.

Stamp Duty on a buy to let property

Stamp duty (or Stamp Duty Land Tax (SDLT) to give it its full name) is payable on a buy to let property. The amount varies depending on the price of the property. The current rates of stamp duty from 1st April 2020 for buy to let properties in England and Northern Ireland are;

- • 3% tax on the first £125,000
- • 5% on the portion up to £250,000
- • 8% on the portion up to £925,000
- • 13% on the portion up to £1.5 million
- • 15% on everything over that

- **In Scotland you'll pay Land and Buildings Transaction Tax**, and the current rates are;
  3% tax on the first £145,000
- 5% on the portion up to £250,000
- 8% on the portion up to £325,000
- 13% on the portion up to £750,000
- 15% on everything over that.

- **In Wales you'll pay Land Transaction Tax**, and the current rates are:
  3% tax on the first £180,000
- 6.5% on the portion up to £250,0008% on the portion up to £400,000
- 10.5% on the portion up to £750,000
- 13% on the portion up to £1,500,000
- 15% on everything over that.

Anyone buying a second property that isn't their main residence will be charged these new rates. This will include holiday lets and buying a property for children if the parents leave their name on the title deeds. Stamp duty has to be paid within 30 days of completion of the purchase of the property although this is usually paid by the solicitor on completion. The amount of Stamp Duty paid is deductible from any capital gains you might make when the property is sold.

Capital Gains Tax (CGT) on buy to let property

If you sell the property for more than you paid for it after deducting costs such as stamp duty and estate agent/solicitors fees you will be liable for CGT. By making a profit, you are essentially 'gaining capital', and so the tax applies. However, as an individual you get an annual allowance to set against any gain. In the 2020/2021tax year, this allowance is £12,000. This is a special allowance purely for capital items and is separate from the annual personal income tax allowance. If the gain is greater than the £12,000 allowance, you will pay tax at a rate of either 18% or 28% on that profit depending on the amount of income and capital gains you have. Note that the lower CGT rates of 10% and 20% announced in the March 2016 budget do not apply to landlords and buy to let properties.

Reducing CGT liability

There are legitimate ways to reduce the amount of Capital Gains Tax (CGT) payable:
- A loss made on the sale of a buy to let property in previous years
- Solicitor fees
- Estate agent fees
- Costs of advertising the property for sale
- Stamp duty
- Any expenditure on 'capital' items

These expenses can be deducted from your capital gain. There are also certain tax reliefs available. For example if the property was previously your main residence, the gain may be reduced.

Like income tax, any gain is declared on your Self Assessment tax return. The tax is therefore payable by the 31st January in the year after the tax year in which the property was sold. (E.g. if a property was sold on 4th May 2020 it is in the tax year to 5th April 2021 so the tax is payable by 31st January 2021.)

However, from April 2019, any tax payable on the profit of the sale of the property will be payable within 30 days of the date the property is sold.

Tax on buy to let property income

The income you receive as rent is taxable. You need to declare any rent you receive as part of your Self Assessment tax return.

The tax on your income is then charged in accordance with your income tax banding (20% for basic rate taxpayers, 40% for higher rate, and 45% for additional rate). However, you can minimise the tax you have to pay by deducting certain 'allowable expenses' from your taxable rental income. Allowable expenses include:

- • Interest on buy to let mortgages and other finance charges (but see below)
- • Council tax, insurance, ground rents etc
- • Property repairs and maintenance – however large improvements such as extensions etc will not be income tax deductible. They will be added to the cost of the property when it is sold and be deductible against any capital gain.
- • Legal, management and other professional fees such as letting agency fees.
- • Other property expenses including buildings insurance premiums

The 2015 Summer Budget has reduced the amount of tax relief that is available for interest on buy to let mortgages from April 2017. Prior to April 2017, tax is payable on your net rental income after deducting allowable expenses including mortgage interest.

This meant that landlords paying higher (40%) or additional (45%) rate tax could claim tax relief at their highest rate. However, from April 2020 tax relief can only be reclaimed at the basic rate (20%), whatever rate of tax the landlord pays. The rules were phased in over 4 years commencing April 2017.

A Worked example of interest deduction new rules
• House is bought for £300,000
• 80% mortgage is taken for £240,000
• Mortgage interest assumed at 4.5% annual mortgage interest is £10,800
• Rental yield is assumed at 5%, annual rent is £15,000

Basic rate taxpayer

	2016/17	2017/18	2018/19	2019/20	2020 on
Annual rental income	£15,000	£15,000	£15,000	£15,000	£15,000
Mortgage interest payable	(£10,800)	(£10,800)	(£10,800)	(£10,800)	(£10,800)
Reduction in mortgage interest allowance*		£2,700	£5,400	£8,100	£10,800
Total rental income on which tax is payable	£4,200	£6,900	£9,600	£12,300	£15,000
Tax at 20%	£840	£1,380	£1,920	£2,460	£3,000
Tax relief at basic rate - 20% of the reduction in mortgage interest allowance		(£540)	(£1,080)	(£1,620)	(£2,160)
Total tax payable	£840	£840	£840	£840	£840

A basic rate tax payer on the face of it will not pay any more tax under the new rules, but that's not the whole story.

The new rules change the way income is calculated. Income is now before deduction of any mortgage interest. In the above example, in 2016-17 (before the new rules), your income was £4,200. In 2020 your income is deemed to be £15,000.

For example, if a person has £35,000 of employment income and rental income of £15,000 and mortgage interest is £10,800.

- Under the old rules the net profit of £4,200 and £35,000 employment income would all be taxed at the lower rate of 20%.
- Under the new rules, from 2020, the income from rental of £15,000 and employment income of £35,000 would even after the personal allowance take the taxpayer into the higher rate tax bracket of 40%. (currently income greater then £42,385). This increase in income could also affect claims for Child Benefit and Income Tax Credits.

The reduction in mortgage interest allowance is 0% in 2016-17, 25% in 2017-18, 50% in 2018-19, 75% in 2019-20, 100% in 2020 and beyond.

Higher rate taxpayer
The tax impact of the new interest deduction rules will be a significant increase to the tax bill for higher rate taxpayers. In 2020, a higher rate tax payer would pay £2,160 more tax.

See table overleaf.

	2016/17	2017/18	2018/19	2019/20	2020 on
Annual rental income	£15,000	£15,000	£15,000	£15,000	£15,000
Mortgage interest payable	(£10,800)	(£10,800)	(£10,800)	(£10,800)	(£10,800)
Reduction in mortgage interest allowance*		£2,700	£5,400	£8,100	£10,800
Total rental income on which tax is payable	£4,200	£6,900	£9,600	£12,300	£15,000
Tax at 40%	£1,680	£2,760	£3,840	£4,920	£6,000
Tax relief at basic rate - 20% of the reduction in mortgage interest allowance		(£540)	(£1,080)	(£1,620)	(£2,160)
Total tax payable	£1,680	£2,200	£2,760	£3,300	£3,840

*The reduction in mortgage interest allowance is 0% in 2016-17, 25% in 2017-18, 50% in 2018-19, 75% in 2019-20, 100% in 2020 and beyond

Using a limited company to minimise tax

There is no simple answer to this. It depends on a number of factors such as how many properties you hold, whether you need the income quickly and how long you want to hold the properties for and your individual circumstances. Limited companies are not affected by the new Mortgage interest relief restriction. Interest for limited companies is classed as a business expense and fully deductible against income. Companies pay corporation tax at a fixed rate irrespective of the size of the profits. The Corporation Tax rate is currently at 20% in 2020. this makes the tax rate very attractive compared to 40% for higher rate tax payers and 45% for additional higher rate taxpayers.

The question is how the money in the company is passed to the individual. If the money is taken out of the company as a dividend, only the first £2,000 of dividend income is tax free. Any dividends taken out in excess of this will either be charged at 7.5% for a basic rate taxpayer 32.5% for a higher rate taxpayer or 38.1% for an additional higher rate taxpayer. This tax is after the corporation tax at 20% has been paid.

The money could be taken as a salary, however the company would have to operate PAYE and pay Employers National insurance contributions on any salaries paid. This usually in most circumstances works out more expensive than paying dividends. Companies do also not benefit from the annual allowance against capital gains. So extracting the money for a sold buy to let property could be less tax efficient than holding the property as an individual. As you have to pay the 20% corporation tax on any gain, no annual allowance is given and you have to pay tax on extracting the money from the company, whereas even a higher rate taxpayer only pays 28% on any gain from the sale of a buy to let as an individual.

Companies also have to prepare accounts to be filed with company's house, prepare and file corporation tax returns which can be more onerous than self-assessment returns.

Interest rates charged on mortgages to companies have historically been higher than to individuals so further investigation of the comparison of the rates charged should be considered alongside the tax implications. Transferring a current buy to let property into a limited company can trigger stamp duty and capital gains tax charges at the time of transfer so advice should be sought before undertaking such a transaction.

Due to the complexities of this area it is essential that you seek proper professional advice.

Inheritance tax on a buy to let property

Inheritance Tax is payable on buy to let properties but the amount changes depending on your circumstances. A buy to let property that you own will form part of your estate for Inheritance Tax purposes. It works like this: if you're operating as a sole landlord – with the buy to let mortgage in your name as an individual and your estate entirely owned by you alone – then you're liable to inheritance tax if your property value less any outstanding mortgage (or combined value of your estate) exceeds £325,000. If you're in this with a married or civil partner, then you each have a threshold of £325,000 so the inheritance tax kicks in at £650,000. Anything above these amounts is taxed at 40%. Inheritance tax planning is complex and definitely something that should be discussed with an expert tax or financial adviser.

Furnished holiday lets

For those landlords who intend to specialise in furnished holiday lets, there are different rules.

What are the 'Furnished Holiday Letting' Tax Rules?

In order for your holiday home to qualify and benefit from the tax rules governing furnished holiday lettings it must first meet all of the following criteria:

- Your holiday home must be located within the European Economic Area (EEA).

- Your holiday home must be let on a commercial basis with a view to making a profit from the lettings.
- Your holiday home must be furnished.

The occupation requirements
There are also several occupation requirements your holiday home will need to meet:

- Your holiday home must be available for at least 210 days (30 weeks) in a 12 month period.
- Your holiday home must be let to the public as holiday accommodation for at least 105 days (15 weeks) in a 12 month period. If your holiday home is new and unable to hit this occupation level it will be taken into consideration.

if your holiday home is occupied by the same guests for more than 31 consecutive days, that 'longer term' form of occupation cannot add up to more than 155 days in a 12 month period.

If you own more than one holiday home, an average would be taken across all of the qualifying properties meaning that if a single property fell beneath the required occupancy threshold it could potentially be buoyed up by other holiday homes that you own.

What if you have a bad year and don't meet the requirements?
In order to continue to qualify as Furnished Holiday Accommodation your holiday home will not need to meet the occupation requirements every year. You will be allowed to miss the thresholds for two consecutive years, with your holiday home ceasing to be

qualify on the third year. This means that as a bare minimum, your holiday home will need to meet the entire occupation requirement at least once every three years.

The benefits of qualifying as Furnished Holiday Letting

There is a wide range of benefits associated with Furnished Holiday Letting Accommodation, which you should discuss with your accountant.

These benefits include:

Profits from furnished holiday lets are deemed "relevant earnings", allowing for tax advantaged pension savings to be made that ordinary letting businesses do not qualify for. Capital allowances can be made on the capital expenditure you make on your holiday home. The first £250,000 of capital expenditure incurred by a person can qualify for 100% Capital Allowances. If you wish to sell your holiday home a range of Capital Gains Tax relief's, usually only available to trading ventures, can be claimed. These could include Entrepreneurs' Relief, Roll-over Relief and Hold-over relief. Many holiday home businesses will be run by a husband and wife team. In this case profits can be allocated in any proportion required, irrespective of their actual shares in the ownership of the property.

****

Useful Websites

The Buying Process
The Local Government Association
www.lga.gov.uk
Confederation of Scottish Local Authorities
www.cosla.gov.uk
Greater London Authority
www.london.gov.uk
The Environment Agency
www.environment-agency.gov.uk
www.homecheckuk.com

House Prices
Halifax www.halifax.co.uk
Nationwide www.nationwide.co.uk
Land Registry www.landreg.gov.uk
www.zoopla.co.uk
www.ourproperty.co.uk
www.upmystreet.com

Property search sites
www.hometrack.co.uk
www.rightmove.co.uk
www.zoopla.co.uk
www.fish4.co.uk
www.findaproperty.com
www.thisislondon.co.uk

The buying and selling process

The Law Society www.lawsoc.org.uk

The Council of Mortgage Lenders www.cml.org.uk

HM Customs and Revenue www.hmrc.gov

Scotland

Law Society of Scotland www.scotlaw.org.uk

Leasehold/freehold

Lease www.lease-advice.org

Association of Residential Managing Agents
www.arma.org.uk

Mortgage search sites/brokers

Money facts www.moneyfacts.co.uk

www.moneysupermarket.co.uk

www.moneynet.co.uk

New homes

NHBC www.nhbc.co.uk

Renting and Letting

Association of Residential Letting Agencies (ARLA Propertymark))

Tel: 01926 496800 Website: www.arla.co.uk Email: info@arla.co.uk

Specialist rental property sites

www.zoopla.co.uk

www.rightmove.co.uk

Auctions
www.propwatch.com
www.primelocation.com
www.bbc.co.uk/homes/property/buying_auction
www.propertyauctions.com

****

A SUMMARY OF IMPORTANT TERMS

FREEHOLDER: Someone who owns their property outright.

LEASEHOLDER: Someone who has been granted permission to live on someone else's land for a fixed term.

TENANCY: One form of lease, the most common types of which are fixed-term or periodic.

LANDLORD: A person who owns the property in which the tenant lives.

LICENCE: A licence is an agreement entered into whereby the landlord is merely giving you permission to occupy his/her property for a limited period of time.

TRESPASSER: Someone who has no right through an agreement to live in a property.

PROTECTED TENANT: In the main, subject to certain exclusions, someone whose tenancy began before 15th January 1989.

ASSURED TENANT: In the main, subject to certain exclusions, someone whose tenancy began after 15th January 1989.

NOTICE TO QUIT: A legal document giving the protected tenant twenty eight days notice that the landlord intends to apply for possession of the property to the County Court.

GROUND FOR POSSESSION: One of the stated reasons for which the landlord can apply for possession of the property.

MANDATORY GROUND: Where the judge must give possession of the property.

DISCRETIONARY GROUND: Where the judge may or may not give possession, depending on his own opinion.

STUDENT LETTING: A tenancy granted by a specified educational institution.

HOLIDAY LETTING: A dwelling used for holiday purposes only.

ASSURED SHORTHOLD TENANCY: A fixed-term post-1989 tenancy.

PAYMENT OF RENT: Where you pay a regular sum of money in return for permission to occupy a property or land for a specified period of time.

FAIR RENT: A rent set by the Rent Officer every two years for most pre-1989 tenancies and is lower than a market rent.

MARKET RENT: A rent deemed to be comparable with other non-fair rents in the area.

RENT ASSESSMENT COMMITTEE: A committee set up to review rents set by either the Rent Officer or the landlord.

PREMIUM: A sum of money charged for permission to live in a property.

DEPOSIT: A sum of money held against the possibility of damage to property.

QUIET ENJOYMENT: The right to live peacefully in your own home.

REPAIRS: Work required to keep a property in good order.

IMPROVEMENTS: Alterations to a property.

LEGAL AID: Help with your legal costs, which is dependent on income.

HOUSING BENEFIT: Financial help with rent, which is dependent on income.

HOUSING ADVICE CENTRE: A center which exists to give advice on housing-related matters and which is usually local authority-funded.

LAW CENTRE: A center, which exists for the purpose of assisting the public with legal advice.

****

Index

****

Appendix 1
A landlord checklist of things to do before tenants move in

➢ Check tenants have the 'Right to Rent' Landlords must ensure tenants can legally reside in the UK before letting to them. The penalty for renting to someone without the right to rent is a £3,000 fine or even imprisonment. The government has issued a list of commonly available documents to check. If your tenants have the right to rent, take a copy of the document and keep it on file.

➢ Protect the deposit. Deposit protection is a legal requirement for landlords. Landlords must protect deposits within 30 days of receiving funds, or face a fine of up to three times the deposit amount.

➢ Make your property fire safe A smoke alarm must be on all floors of the property, and carbon monoxide detectors must be in any rooms with fuel-burning devices. If your property comes with furniture, it should be flame resistant.

➢ Make sure your Gas Safety Certificate is up to date If there's a gas supply at the property, you must arrange a gas safety inspection each year. (Ideally, You must give a copy of the certificate to tenants at the start of a tenancy).

➢ Make sure your EPC is up to date Landlords must have a valid EPC (Energy Performance Certificate) to let a property legally in the UK. You must give a copy of the certificate to tenants at the start of a tenancy.

➢ Give tenants a copy of the 'How to Rent' guide This guide lists landlord obligations and tenants' rights. You must either give tenants a hard copy or email it to them as an attachment. A link to the guide is not enough.

➤ Landlords who fail to do this are unable to evict tenants under a Section 21 Notice.

➤ Make sure appliances are in working order Any appliance left in the property must be safe to use. Anything not working should be replaced or removed.

You should also:

➤ Reference your tenants This is the best insight into your tenant's ability to pay their rent on time. A good referencing service will check affordability, employability, credit history, and a previous landlord reference.

➤ Prepare an inventory Although not a legal requirement, an inventory is vital for getting funds from the deposit. If tenants disagree with your deductions, you won't be able to claim anything without a signed inventory.

➤ Take meter readings This keeps things fair. It means tenants will know what they're responsible to pay, and helps prevent landlords from being left with outstanding payments.

➤ Update utility suppliers It's a good idea to update utility suppliers with new tenant details. This ensures any utilities tenants use will be billed to them.

➤ Provide emergency contact numbers Important — especially for minimising any damage caused to the property.

➤ If a pipe bursts in the middle of the night, for example, your tenants need to know who to call.

➤ Change the locks Some might view this as an additional expense, but it could be essential for the safety of your new tenants. If you don't change the locks, you must be confident your previous tenants were trustworthy enough to return all copies of the keys.

Appendix 2

Sample Assured Shorthold Tenancy Agreement (England and Wales) with inventory

Sample Notices Requiring Possession England and Wales (Form 6A plus notes and Form 3)

ASSURED SHORTHOLD TENANCY AGREEMENT ENGLAND AND WALES

This Tenancy Agreement is between

Name and address of Landlord-

-AND

Name of tenant:

the Tenant"

(in the case of Joint Tenants the term "Tenant" applies to each of them and the names of all Joint Tenants should be written above. Each Tenant individually has the full responsibilities and rights set out in this Agreement)

Address-in respect of:

("the Premises")

Description of Premises

-

Which comprises of:

Term-The Tenancy is granted for a fixed term of [6] months

Date of start of tenancy-The Tenancy begins on:

("The Commencement Date") and is an assured shorthold monthly tenancy, the terms of which are set out in this Agreement.

Overcrowding-The Tenant agrees not to allow any person other than the Tenant to reside at the Premises.

Payment of Deposit-The Tenant agrees to pay on signing the Agreement a deposit of £   which will be returnable in full providing that the Landlord may deduct from such sums: The reasonable costs of any necessary repairs to the premises, building or common parts, or the replacement of any or all of the contents where such repair or replacement is due to any act or omission of the Tenant or family or visitors of the Tenant, such sums as are outstanding on leaving the Premises in respect of arrears or other charges including Court costs or other fees.

The deposit will be protected by The Deposit Protection Service (The DPS) in accordance with the Terms and Conditions of The DPS. The Terms and Conditions and ADR Rules governing the protection of the deposit including the repayment process can be found at www.depositprotection.com

Payment for the premises-

Rent: The rent for the premises is:

      Service Charge:

      Total:

In this Agreement the term "Rent" refers to the net rent and service charge set out above or as varied from time to time in accordance with this Agreement.

The payment of monthly Rent is due in advance on the first Saturday of each month.

The service charge is in respect of the landlord providing the services listed in Schedule 1 to this Agreement for which the Tenant shall pay a service charge to be included in the rent. The service charge may be varied by the landlord in accordance with the terms set out in Schedule 1 to this Agreement.

I/We have read, understood and accept the terms and conditions contained within this agreement which include the standard terms and conditions attached.

Signed by the Tenant

.... Dated:

Signed on behalf of the landlord

.... Dated:

If the Tenant feels that the landlord has broken this Agreement or not performed any obligation contained in it, he/she should first complain to the landlord in writing giving details of the breach or non-performance.

Terms and Conditions

1. It is agreed that:

Changes in Rent-1.1-The landlord may increase or decrease the Rent by giving the Tenant not less than 4 weeks notice in writing of the increase or decrease.

The notice shall specify the Rent proposed. The first increase or decrease shall be on the first day of   following the Commencement Date of this Agreement. Subsequent increases or decreases in the Rent shall take effect on the first day of   in each subsequent year.

The revised Rent shall be the amount specified in the notice of increase unless the Tenant exercises his/her right to refer the notice to a Rent Assessment Committee to have a market rent determined in which case the maximum Rent payable for one year after the date specified in the notice shall be the Rent so determined.

Altering the Agreement-1.2-With the exception of any changes in Rent, this Agreement may only be altered by the agreement in writing of both the Tenant and the landlord.

2. The landlord agrees:

Possession-2.1-To give the Tenant possession of the Premises at the commencement of the Tenancy.
Tenant's Right to Occupy-2.2-Not to interrupt or interfere with the Tenant's right peacefully to occupy the Premises except where:

(i)   access is required to inspect the condition of the Premises or to carry out repairs or other works to the Premises or adjoining property; or

(ii)   a court has given the Association possession by ending the Tenancy.

Repair of Structure and Exterior-2.3-To keep in good repair the structure and exterior of the Premises including:

- drains, gutters and external pipes;
- the roof;
- outside wall, outside doors, windowsills, window catches, sash cords and window frames including necessary external painting and decorating;
- internal walls, floors and ceilings, doors and door frames, door hinges and skirting boards but not including internal painting and decoration;
- plasterwork;
- chimneys, chimney stacks and flues but not including sweeping;
- pathways, steps or other means of access;
- integral garages and stores;
- boundary walls and fences.

Repair of Installations-2.4-To keep in good repair and working order any installations provided by the landlord for space heating, water heating and sanitation and for the supply of water, gas and electricity including:

- o basins, sinks, baths, toilets, flushing systems and waste pipes;
- o electric wiring including sockets and switches, gas pipes and water pipes;
- o water heaters, fireplaces, fitted fires and central heating installations

Repair of Common Parts-2.5-To take reasonable care to keep the common entrances, halls, stairways, lifts, passageways, rubbish chutes and any other common parts, including their lighting, in reasonable repair and fit for use by the Tenant and other occupiers and visitors to the Premises.

External & Internal Decorations-2.6-To keep the exterior and interior of the Premises and any common parts in a good state of decoration and normally to decorate these areas once every 5 years.

3. The Tenant agrees:

Possession-3.1-To take possession of the Premises at the commencement of the Tenancy and not to part with possession of the Premises or sub-let the whole or part of it.

Rent-3.2-To pay the Rent monthly and in advance. The first payment shall be made on the signing of the Agreement in respect of the period from the Commencement Date to the first Saturday of the following month.

Use of Premises-3.3-To use the Premises for residential purposes as the Tenant's only or principal home and not to operate a business at the Premises without the written consent of the landlord.

Nuisance and Racial and other Harassment-3.4-Not to behave or allow members of his/her household or any other person visiting the Premises with the Tenant's permission to behave in a manner nor do anything which is likely to be a nuisance to the tenants, owners or lessees of any of the other properties or other persons lawfully visiting the property.

In particular, not to cause any interference, nuisance or annoyance through noise, anti-social behaviour or threats of or actual violence or any damage to property belonging to the said persons. This Clause also applies to any conduct or activity which amounts to harassment including: abuse and intimidation, creating unacceptable levels of noise or causing intentional damage or any other persistent behaviour which causes offence, discomfort or inconvenience on the grounds of colour, race religion, sex, sexual orientation and disability.

Noise Not to allow be played any radio, television, audio equipment or musical instrument so loudly that it causes a nuisance or annoyance to neighbours or can be heard outside the Premises.

Domestic Violence-3.6-Not to use or threaten violence against any other person living in the Premises such that they are forced to leave by reason of the Tenant's violence or fear of such violence.

Pets-3.7-To keep under control any animals at the Premises and to obtain the written consent of the landlord before keeping a dog or any other animal.

Car Repairs-3.8-That no car servicing or car repairs shall be carried out in the roads or accessway or parking spaces or in the forecourt or approaches to the Premises, such as to be a nuisance or annoyance to neighbours.

Paraffin-3.9-Not to use any paraffin or bottled gas heating, lighting or cooking appliances on the Premises nor any appliances which discharge the products of combustion into the interior of the Premises.

Vehicles-3.10-That no commercial vehicle, caravan, boat, or lorry shall be parked in the accessway or parking spaces.

(regardless of whether this forms part of the Premises) or in the forecourt or approaches to the Premises or the adjoining premises.

Keeping premises clean-3.11-To keep the interior of the Premises in a clean condition. The Tenant agrees to return the property in the same decorative order as at the start of the tenancy taking into account fair wear and tear.

Damage-3.12-To make good any damage caused willfully or by neglect or carelessness on the part of the Tenant or any member of the Tenant's household or visitor to the Premises.

This includes the replacement of any broken glass in windows and repair or replacement of any damaged fittings and installations. If the Tenant fails to make good any damage for which he/she is responsible the landlord may enter the Premises and carry out the work in default and the cost of this work shall be recoverable by the Association from the Tenant.

Reporting Disrepair-3.13-To report to the landlord any disrepair or defect for which the landlord is responsible in the structure or exterior of the Premises or in any installation therein or in the common parts.

Access-3.14-To allow the landlords employees or contractors acting on behalf of the landlord access at all reasonable hours of the daytime to inspect the condition of the Premises or to carry out repairs or other works to the Premises or adjoining property. The landlord will normally give at least 24 hours' notice, but immediate access may be required and shall be given in an emergency.

Assignment-3.15-Not to assign the Tenancy.

Sub-Tenants-3.16-Not to sub-let the whole or part of the Premises.

Ending the Tenancy-3.17-To give the landlord at least [4] weeks notice in writing when the Tenant wishes to end the Tenancy.

Moving Out-3.18-To give the landlord vacant possession and return the keys of the Premises at the end of the Tenancy and to remove all personal possessions and rubbish and leave the Premises and the landlords furniture and fixtures in good lettable condition and repair. The landlord accepts no responsibility for anything left at the Premises by the Tenant at the end of the Tenancy.

4. The Tenant has the following rights:

Right to Occupy-4.1-The Tenant has the right to occupy the Premises without interruption or interference from the landlord for the duration of this Tenancy (except for the obligation contained in this Agreement to give access to the landlords employees or contractors) so long as the Tenant complies with the terms of this Agreement and has proper respect for the rights of other tenants and neighbours.

Security of Tenure-4.2-The Tenant has security of tenure as an assured tenant so long as he/she occupies the Premises as his/her only or principal home. Before the expiry of the fixed term the landlord can only end the Tenancy by obtaining a court order for possession of the Premises on one of the grounds listed in Schedule 2 of the Housing Act 1988. The landlord will only use the following grounds to obtain an order for possession

- The tenant has not paid rent which is due; (Ground 10)
- The Tenant has broken, or failed to perform, any of the conditions of this Tenancy; (Ground 12)

- The Tenant or anyone living in the premises has caused damage to, or failed to look after the premises, the building, any of the common parts; (Ground 13)
- The Tenant or anyone living in the premises has caused serious or persistent nuisance or annoyance to neighbours, or has been responsible for any act of harassment on the grounds of race, colour, religion, sex, sexual orientation, or disability, or has been convicted of using the property for immoral or illegal purposes; (Ground 14) or because of domestic violence (Ground 14A)
- Where the tenancy has devolved under the will or intestacy of the Tenant
- Suitable alternative accommodation is available to the Tenant

Notice Periods for ending Assured Tenancy-4.3-Before the expiry of the fixed term the landlord agrees that it will not give less than four weeks notice in writing of its intention to seek a possession order except where it is seeking possession on Ground 14 or Ground 14A (whether or not combined with other Grounds) where it shall give such period of notice that it shall decide and that is not less than the statutory minimum notice period

Expiry of Tenancy-4.4-The landlord can only end the Tenancy by giving the Tenant at least two months notice that it requires possession of the Premises and by obtaining a court order for possession. The court will make an order for possession if it is satisfied that the proper notice has been given.

Cessation of Assured Tenancy-4.5-If the Tenancy ceases to be an assured tenancy the landlord may end the Tenancy by giving four weeks' notice in writing which shall be validly served on the Tenant if posted or delivered to the Premises.

****

**Department for
Communities and
Local Government**

FORM 6A
Notice seeking possession of a property
let on an Assured Shorthold Tenancy

Housing Act 1988 section 21(1) and (4) as amended by section 194 and paragraph 103 of Schedule 11 to the Local Government and Housing Act 1989 and section 98(2) and (3) of the Housing Act 1996

Please write clearly in black ink. Please tick boxes where appropriate.

This form should be used where a no fault possession of accommodation let under an assured shorthold tenancy (AST) is sought under section 21(1) or (4) of the Housing Act 1988.

There are certain circumstances in which the law says that you cannot seek possession against your tenant using section 21 of the Housing Act 1988, in which case you should not use this form. These are:

(a) during the first four months of the tenancy (but where the tenancy is a replacement tenancy, the four month period is calculated by reference to the start of the original tenancy and not the start of the replacement tenancy – see section 21(4B) of the Housing Act 1988);

(b) where the landlord is prevented from retaliatory eviction under section 33 of the Deregulation Act 2015;

(c) where the landlord has not provided the tenant with an energy performance certificate, gas safety certificate or the Department for Communities and Local Government's publication "How to rent: the checklist for renting in England" (see the Assured Shorthold Tenancy Notices and Prescribed Requirements (England) Regulations 2015);

(d) where the landlord has not complied with the tenancy deposit protection legislation; or

(e) where a property requires a licence but is unlicensed.

Landlords who are unsure about whether they are affected by these provisions should seek specialist advice.

This form must be used for all ASTs created on or after 1 October 2015 except for statutory periodic tenancies which have come into being on or after 1 October 2015 at the end of fixed term ASTs created before 1 October 2015. There is no obligation to use this form in relation to ASTs created prior to 1 October 2015, however it may nevertheless be used for all ASTs.

What to do if this notice is served on you

You should read this notice very carefully. It explains that your landlord has started the process to regain possession of the property referred to in section 2 below.

You are entitled to at least two months' notice before being required to give up possession of the property. However, if your tenancy started on a periodic basis without any initial fixed term a longer notice period may be required depending on how often you are required to pay rent (for example, if you pay rent quarterly, you must be given at least three months' notice, or, if you have a periodic tenancy which is half yearly or annual, you must be given at least six months' notice (which is the maximum)). The date you are required to leave should be shown in section 2 below. After this date the landlord can apply to court for a possession order against you.

Where your tenancy is terminated before the end of a period of your tenancy (e.g. where you pay rent in advance on the first of each month and you are required to give up possession in the middle of the month), you may be entitled to repayment of rent from the landlord under section 21C of the Housing Act 1988.

If you need advice about this notice, and what you should do about it, take it immediately to a citizens' advice bureau, a housing advice centre, a law centre or a solicitor.

To:

Name(s) of tenant(s) (Block Capitals)

You are required to leave the below address after [   ] [1]. If you do not leave, your landlord may apply to the court for an order under section 21(1) or (4) of the Housing Act 1988 requiring you to give up possession.

Address of premises

---

[1] Landlords should insert a calendar date here. The date should allow sufficient time to ensure that the notice is properly served on the tenant(s). This will depend on the method of service being used and landlords should check whether the tenancy agreement makes specific provision about service. Where landlords are seeking an order for possession on a periodic tenancy under section 21(4) of the Housing Act 1988, the notice period should also not be shorter than the period of the tenancy (up to a maximum of six months), e.g. where there is a quarterly periodic tenancy, the date should be three months from the date of service.

2

3. This notice is valid for six months only from the date of issue unless you have a periodic tenancy under which more than two months' notice is required (see notes accompanying this form) in which case this notice is valid for four months only from the date specified in section 2 above.

4. Name and address of landlord

To be signed and dated by the landlord or their agent (someone acting for them). If there are joint landlords each landlord or the agent should sign unless one signs on behalf of the rest with their agreement.

Signed

Date (DD/MM/YYYY)

Please specify whether: ☐ landlord ☐ joint landlords ☐ landlord's agent

Name(s) of signatory/signatories (Block Capitals)

Address(es) of signatory/signatories

Telephone of signatory/signatories

Form 6A

Department for
Communities and
Local Government

Notice seeking possession of a property let on an Assured Shorthold Tenancy (Form 6a)

This form should be used where a no fault possession of accommodation let under an assured shorthold tenancy (AST) is sought under section 21(1) or (4) of the Housing Act 1988.

This form must be used for all ASTs created on or after 1 October 2015 except for statutory periodic tenancies which have come into being on or after 1 October 2015 at the end of fixed term ASTs created before 1 October 2015.

The validity period of this form is six months following the date of its issue unless the tenancy is a periodic tenancy under which more than two months' notice is required, in which case the validity period is four months from the date the tenant is required to leave (see notes accompanying the form).

You cannot use this form:

> in the first four months of the tenancy (but where the tenancy is a replacement tenancy, the four month period is calculated by reference to the start of the original tenancy and not the start of the replacement tenancy – see section 21(4B) of the Housing Act 1988);
>
> where the landlord is prevented from retaliatory eviction under section 33 of the Deregulation Act 2015;
>
> where the landlord has not provided the prescribed information and/or prescribed documents as set out below;
>
> where the landlord has not complied with the tenancy deposit protection legislation; or
>
> where a property requires a licence but is unlicensed.

Prescribed Information

The landlord is required to provide a copy of the Department for Communities and Local Government's publication "How to rent: the checklist for renting in England" by providing a pdf copy (which may be obtained from www.gov.uk/government/publications/how-to-rent). We recommend that this should be given at the start of the tenancy. Landlords are not required to supply a further copy of the publication each time a different version is published during the tenancy.

Where the landlord has failed to provide the publication, this form may not be used. However, this restriction is lifted as soon as the publication has been provided.

The requirement does not apply where a landlord is a private registered provider of social housing or where a landlord has already provided the tenant with an up-to-date version of the booklet under an earlier tenancy.

If the tenant has not notified the landlord, or a person acting on behalf of the landlord, of an e-mail address at which the tenant is content to accept service of notices and other documents given under or in connection with the tenancy, the landlord must provide a paper copy of the publication.

Prescribed documents:

Where the landlord has failed to comply with certain existing legal obligations, this form may not be used. However, this restriction is lifted as soon as the obligations have been complied with. The obligations are the requirement on a landlord to provide the tenant with:

- an Energy Performance Certificate (Reg 6(5), The Energy Performance of Buildings (England and Wales) Regulations 2012); and
- a gas safety certificate (Reg 36(6)(a), The Gas Safety (Installation and Use) Regulations 1998)

Tenants that need advice about this notice, and what to do about it, should take it immediately to a citizens' advice bureau, a housing advice centre, a law centre or a solicitor.

Tenants can also get expert, independent advice free from Shelterline on 0808 800 4444. Their advisers will be able to give expert advice, independent advice.

FORM 3

Notice seeking possession of a property let on an Assured Tenancy or an Assured Agricultural Occupancy

Housing Act 1988 section 8 as amended by section 151 of the Housing Act 1996, section 97 of the Anti-social Behaviour, Crime and Policing Act 2014, and section 41 of the Immigration Act 2016.

- Please write clearly in black ink.
- Please cross out text marked with an asterisk (*) that does not apply.
- This form should be used where possession of accommodation let under an assured tenancy, an assured agricultural occupancy or an assured shorthold tenancy is sought on one of the grounds in Schedule 2 to the Housing Act 1988.
- Do not use this form if possession is sought on the "shorthold" ground under section 21 of the Housing Act 1988 from an assured shorthold tenant where the fixed term has come to an end or, for assured shorthold tenancies with no fixed term which started on or after 28th February 1997, after six months has elapsed. Form 6A 'Notice seeking possession of a property let on an Assured Shorthold Tenancy' is prescribed for these cases.

1   To:..

Name(s) of tenant(s)/licensee(s) *

2   Your landlord/licensor* intends to apply to the court for an order requiring you to give up possession of:..............
....
....

Address of premises

3   Your landlord/licensor* intends to seek possession on ground(s) .... in Schedule 2 to the Housing Act 1988 (as amended), which read(s): ....
....
....

Give the full text (as set out in the Housing Act 1988 (as amended) of each ground which is being relied on. Continue on a separate sheet if necessary.

4   Give a full explanation of why each ground is being relied on: ....
....
....

Continue on a separate sheet if necessary.

Notes on the grounds for possession

- If the court is satisfied that any of grounds 1 to 8 is established, it must make an order (but see below in respect of fixed term tenancies).
- Before the court will grant an order on any of grounds 9 to 17, it must be satisfied that it is reasonable to require you to leave. This means that, if one of these grounds is set out in section 3, you will be able to suggest to the court that it is not reasonable that you should have to leave, even if you accept that the ground applies.
- The court will not make an order under grounds 1, 3 to 6[1], 9 or 16, to take effect during the fixed term of the tenancy (if there is one) and it will only make an order during the fixed term on grounds 2, 7, 7A, 8, 10 to 15 or 17 if the terms of the tenancy make provision for it to be brought to an end on any of these

---

[1] Amended to reflect changes shortly to be made to correct the form prescribed in the Assured Tenancies and Agricultural Occupancies (Forms) (England) Regulations 2015.

grounds. It may make an order for possession on ground 7B during a fixed-term of the tenancy even if the terms of the tenancy do not make provision for it to be brought to an end on this ground.

- Where the court makes an order for possession solely on ground 6 or 9, the landlord must pay your reasonable removal expenses.

5   The court proceedings will not begin until after: ....
....

Give the earliest date on which court proceedings can be brought

Notes on the earliest date on which court proceedings can be brought

- Where the landlord is seeking possession on grounds 1, 2, 5 to 7, 9 or 16 (without ground 7A or 14), court proceedings cannot begin earlier than 2 months from the date this notice is served on you and not before the date on which the tenancy (had it not been assured) could have been brought to an end by a notice to quit served at the same time as this notice. This applies even if one of grounds 3, 4, 7B, 8, 10 to 13, 14ZA, 14A, 15 or 17 is also specified.

- Where the landlord is seeking possession on grounds 3, 4, 7B, 8, 10 to 13, 14ZA, 14A, 15 or 17 (without ground 7A or 14), court proceedings cannot begin earlier than 2 weeks from the date this notice is served. If one of 1, 2, 5 to 7, 9 or 16 grounds is also specified court proceedings cannot begin earlier than two months from the date this notice is served.

- Where the landlord is seeking possession on ground 7A (with or without other grounds), court proceedings cannot begin earlier than 1 month from the date this notice is served on you and not before the date on which the tenancy (had it not been assured) could have been brought to an end by a notice to quit served at the same time as this notice. A notice seeking possession on ground 7A must be served on you within specified time periods which vary depending on which condition is relied upon:

  o   Where the landlord proposes to rely on condition 1, 3 or 5: within 12 months of the conviction (or if the conviction is appealed: within 12 months of the conclusion of the appeal);

  o   Where the landlord proposes to rely on condition 2: within 12 months of the court's finding that the injunction has been breached (or if the finding is appealed: within 12 months of the conclusion of the appeal);

  o   Where the landlord proposes to rely on condition 4: within 3 months of the closure order (or if the order is appealed: within 3 months of the conclusion of the appeal).

- Where the landlord is seeking possession on ground 14 (with or without other grounds other than ground 7A), court proceedings cannot begin before the date this notice is served.

- Where the landlord is seeking possession on ground 14A, court proceedings cannot begin unless the landlord has served, or has taken all reasonable steps to serve, a copy of this notice on the partner who has left the property.

- After the date shown in section 5, court proceedings may be begun at once but not later than 12 months from the date on which this notice is served. After this time the notice will lapse and a new notice must be served before possession can be sought.

6   Name and address of landlord/licensor*.

To be signed and dated by the landlord or licensor or the landlord's or licensor's agent (someone acting for the landlord or licensor). If there are joint landlords each landlord or the agent must sign unless one signs on behalf of the rest with their agreement.

Signed .... Date ....
....
....

Please specify whether: landlord / licensor / joint landlords / landlord's agent

Name(s) (Block Capitals).. ....
....

Address ....
....
....

Telephone: Daytime .... *Evening* ....

What to do if this notice is served on you

- This notice is the first step requiring you to give up possession of your home. You should read it very carefully.

- Your landlord cannot make you leave your home without an order for possession issued by a court. By issuing this notice your landlord is informing you that he intends to seek such an order. If you are willing to give up possession without a court order, you should tell the person who signed this notice as soon as possible and say when you are prepared to leave.

- Whichever grounds are set out in section 3 of this form, the court may allow any of the other grounds to be added at a later date. If this is done, you will be told about it so you can discuss the additional grounds at the court hearing as well as the grounds set out in section 3.

- If you need advice about this notice, and what you should do about it, take it immediately to a citizens' advice bureau, a housing advice centre, a law centre or a solicitor.